W9-AUY-388

Death and Dying

Other Books of Related Interest:

At Issue Series

AIDS in Developing Countries

The Right to Die

What Motivates Suicide Bombers?

Current Controversies Series

Resistant Infections

Global Viewpoints Series

Population Growth

Introducing Issues with Opposing Viewpoints Series

Death and Dying

The Death Penalty

Euthanasia

Opposing Viewpoints Series

Health

Social Issues in Literature

Genocide in Elie Wiesel's *Night*

GLOBALVIEWPOINTS

Death and Dying

Diane Andrews Henningfeld, Book Editor

GREENHAVEN PRESS
A part of Gale, Cengage Learning

GALE
CENGAGE Learning™

Detroit • New York • San Francisco • New Haven, Conn • Waterville, Maine • London

GALE
CENGAGE Learning™

Christine Nasso, *Publisher*
Elizabeth Des Chenes, *Managing Editor*

© 2010 Greenhaven Press, a part of Gale, Cengage Learning

Gale and Greenhaven Press are registered trademarks used herein under license.

For more information, contact:
Greenhaven Press
27500 Drake Rd.
Farmington Hills, MI 48331-3535
Or you can visit our Internet site at gale.cengage.com

ALL RIGHTS RESERVED.
No part of this work covered by the copyright herein may be reproduced, transmitted, stored, or used in any form or by any means graphic, electronic, or mechanical, including but not limited to photocopying, recording, scanning, digitizing, taping, Web distribution, information networks, or information storage and retrieval systems, except as permitted under Section 107 or 108 of the 1976 United States Copyright Act, without the prior written permission of the publisher.

For product information and technology assistance, contact us at

Gale Customer Support, 1-800-877-4253
For permission to use material from this text or product, submit all requests online at www.cengage.com/permissions

Further permissions questions can be emailed to permissionrequest@cengage.com

Articles in Greenhaven Press anthologies are often edited for length to meet page requirements. In addition, original titles of these works are changed to clearly present the main thesis and to explicitly indicate the author's opinion. Every effort is made to ensure that Greenhaven Press accurately reflects the original intent of the authors. Every effort has been made to trace the owners of copyrighted material.

Cover image © Abed Al Hashlamoun/epa/Corbis.

LIBRARY OF CONGRESS CATALOGING-IN-PUBLICATION DATA

Death and dying / Diane Andrews Henningfeld, book editor.
   p. cm. -- (Global viewpoints)
   Includes bibliographical references and index.
   ISBN 978-0-7377-4931-1 (hardcover) -- ISBN 978-0-7377-4932-8 (pbk.)
   1. Mortality--Case studies. 2. Death--Social aspects--Case studies. 3. Death--Religious aspects--Case studies. 4. Terminal care--Case studies. I. Henningfeld, Diane Andrews.
   HB1321.D43 2010
   304.6'4--dc22
                                     2010004545

Printed in the United States of America
1 2 3 4 5 6 7 14 13 12 11 10

Contents

Chapter 2: End-of-Life Care

Chapter 3: Death, Dying, and Religion

Chapter 4: Funeral Practices Throughout the World

Foreword

> *"The problems of all of humanity can*
> *only be solved by all of humanity."*
> —*Swiss author Friedrich Dürrenmatt*

Global interdependence has become an undeniable reality. Mass media and technology have increased worldwide access to information and created a society of global citizens. Understanding and navigating this global community is a challenge, requiring a high degree of information literacy and a new level of learning sophistication.

Building on the success of its flagship series, *Opposing Viewpoints*, Greenhaven Press has created the *Global Viewpoints* series to examine a broad range of current, often controversial topics of worldwide importance from a variety of international perspectives. Providing students and other readers with the information they need to explore global connections and think critically about worldwide implications, each *Global Viewpoints* volume offers a panoramic view of a topic of widespread significance.

Drugs, famine, immigration—a broad, international treatment is essential to do justice to social, environmental, health, and political issues such as these. Junior high, high school, and early college students, as well as general readers, can all use *Global Viewpoints* anthologies to discern the complexities relating to each issue. Readers will be able to examine unique national perspectives while, at the same time, appreciating the interconnectedness that global priorities bring to all nations and cultures.

Material in each volume is selected from a diverse range of sources, including journals, magazines, newspapers, nonfiction books, speeches, government documents, pamphlets, organization newsletters, and position papers. *Global Viewpoints* is truly global, with material drawn primarily from international sources available in English and secondarily from U.S. sources with extensive international coverage.

Features of each volume in the *Global Viewpoints* series include:

- An **annotated table of contents** that provides a brief summary of each essay in the volume, including the name of the country or area covered in the essay.

- An **introduction** specific to the volume topic.

- A **world map** to help readers locate the countries or areas covered in the essays.

- For each viewpoint, an **introduction** that contains notes about the author and source of the viewpoint explains why material from the specific country is being presented, summarizes the main points of the viewpoint, and offers three **guided reading questions** to aid in understanding and comprehension.

- **For further discussion** questions that promote critical thinking by asking the reader to compare and contrast aspects of the viewpoints or draw conclusions about perspectives and arguments.

- A worldwide list of **organizations to contact** for readers seeking additional information.

- A **periodical bibliography** for each chapter and a **bibliography of books** on the volume topic to aid in further research.

- A comprehensive **subject index** to offer access to people, places, events, and subjects cited in the text, with the countries covered in the viewpoints highlighted.

Global Viewpoints is designed for a broad spectrum of readers who want to learn more about current events, history, political science, government, international relations, economics, environmental science, world cultures, and sociology—students doing research for class assignments or debates, teachers and faculty seeking to supplement course materials, and others wanting to understand current issues better. By presenting how people in various countries perceive the root causes, current consequences, and proposed solutions to worldwide challenges, *Global Viewpoints* volumes offer readers opportunities to enhance their global awareness and their knowledge of cultures worldwide.

Introduction

The discipline of logic offers an oft-quoted syllogism concerning humans and mortality: "All men are mortal. Socrates is a man. Therefore, Socrates is mortal." With these words, the ancients not only illustrated logical reasoning, but they also made an important statement about the human condition: No one escapes death. Every human being, without exception, will die.

Although death is common to every living thing, no experience is more mysterious, more puzzling. No one who has experienced death remains to write self-help books or serve as talk show guests. The living are left to wonder what happens, if anything, at the moment of death. As Hamlet ponders in William Shakespeare's great play, death is "The undiscover'd country, from whose bourn / No traveller returns."

Belief systems, religion, and cultural rituals, however, have helped the dying and their families cope with the great unknown of death. Many people believe that their lives will continue in another form after death or that they will go to heaven. Religious rituals and rites offer comfort and structure to the transition from living to death.

While nearly every culture has rituals or customs concerning death and the treatment of the dead, these rituals vary widely across the globe. It can be a challenge for individuals raised in one culture to understand or embrace the traditions of other cultures, particularly in the emotionally fraught, taboo-ridden realm of the disposal of human remains.

Westerners, for the most part, dispose of human remains in one of two ways: burial or cremation. While these two methods are common throughout the world, several other cultural customs exist. Excarnation, or exposing the dead body to predators or the elements, is one such tradition. The Australian Museum's Web site Death – The Last Taboo (http://

australianmuseum.net.au/Death-The-Last-Taboo) reminds readers that "in many cultures [excarnation] is the desired disposal method—one which is natural, efficient and which counters the waste and earthly contamination of other methods." They add that this was a common practice among indigenous peoples in Australia and North America, who would then retrieve the skeletal remains for burial.

Various forms of excarnation are used today. Tibetan Buddhists, for example, practice an ancient tradition called "sky burial." When a person dies, the body is left unpreserved and untouched for three days while attended to by lamas, or monks, who perform ritual prayers. This is also the time of mourning and grieving by the family of the deceased. They believe that the soul leaves the body in stages before being released to a new life through reincarnation, or, the most hoped for possibility, the soul achieves nirvana, or enlightenment, when the cycle of endless reincarnation ceases.

After the ritual three days, the lamas move the body to a mountainside sacred location where large vultures gather in anticipation, held back by other lamas. Family members, friends, and monks accompany the body. At the appointed time, one of the lamas sharpens a large knife and then begins dismembering the body, cutting the flesh into big chunks. Then he uses a large hammer to crush the bones. When he is finished, the vultures are released and they quickly devour the entire body before flying away.

As the vultures' droppings reach the earth, the cycle of reincarnation for the departed soul begins again. In a 1999 *Seattle Post-Intelligencer* article, "Tibet's 'Sky-Burial' Lives on to Link Death and Nature," the newspaper quotes a Tibetan monk called Garloji who explains, "When the body dies, the spirit leaves, so there is no need to keep the body. . . . The birds, they think they are just eating. Actually, they are removing the body and completing part of life's cycle."

A moving description of one such sky burial comes from Rachel Laribee, who witnessed the custom while visiting Tibet as a college student. In "Tibetan Sky Burial," an article that appeared in the *River Gazette* in 2005, Laribee offers a detailed account of what she saw, revealing, "Even though I am very familiar with Tibetan culture and practices, I must confess that at first, I was still dismayed that this culture that I had grown to love would treat their dead as if they were nothing more than lunch meat." After some reflection, however, Laribee realized the sky burial was not disrespectful nor sad: "I looked at the faces of the family. . . . There were no signs of horror on their faces, nor any hint of tears. . . . The tears and the mourning are completed earlier during the three days of prayers. . . . The function of the sky burial is simply the disposal of the body."

In addition to the Tibetan religious belief that the body is simply a borrowed vessel for the soul and that it must be returned to the elements of the earth, the climate and terrain of Tibet make sky burial not only appropriate but also necessary. In this mountainous, cold region, timber and fuel are scarce, and they must be used to heat homes and cook food. Thus, a funeral pyre or cremation would be inordinately expensive and a waste of precious resources. In Tibet, the ground is frozen for most of the year, and below a thin layer of dirt is solid rock. Burial in such terrain is nearly impossible.

Scientists laud the practice of sky burial for being one of the most environmentally sound ways of disposing of the dead. Cremation uses carbon-based fuels, leading to increased global warming. In addition, dangerous mercury vapors from dental fillings pollute the air during cremation. Burial can also be an environmentally damaging tradition. Embalming fluids and other pollutants can seep into the earth when corpses are buried, contaminating the soil and the water table. In "Death Can Be Good for the Soul," an article that appeared in the March 18, 1999, issue of the *Evening News* in Edinburgh, Scotland, Graham Tibbetts interviewed David Pescod, an English scientist who studies death. Pescod argues that sky burial is not only an enlightened, environmentally sound method of corpse disposal, but also the "ultimate in recycling."

Learning about death and dying across cultures can be informative, interesting, and educational, helping individuals understand not only the dead, but also the living in all parts of the world. The viewpoints that follow delve into topics that are both controversial and difficult, asking readers to consider issues such as violence, euthanasia, suicide, end-of-life care, and varying religious and cultural customs.

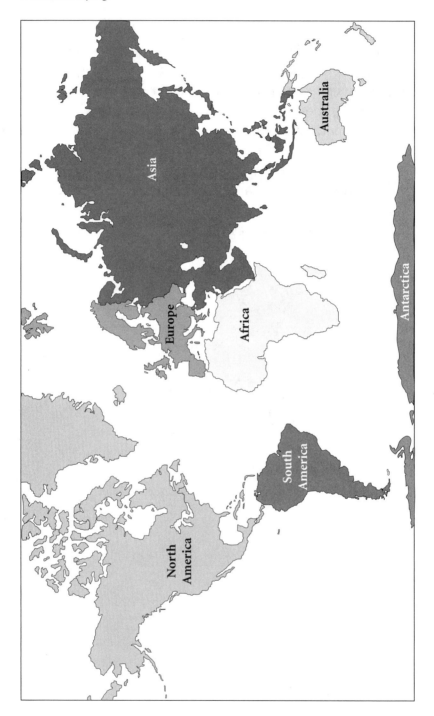

GLOBALVIEWPOINTS

CHAPTER 1

Causes of
Death Worldwide

In Africa, Many Die from AIDS

Annabel Kanabus, Jenni Fredriksson-Bass, and Graham Pembrey

In the following viewpoint, Annabel Kanabus, Jenni Fredriksson-Bass, and Graham Pembrey report on the status of HIV/AIDS in sub-Saharan Africa, an area that suffers more HIV/AIDS deaths than any other location in the world. According to the authors, major effects include a reduction in life expectancy, loss of income earners in many homes, strain on health care, damage to education, reduced productivity, and slowed economic growth. Greater funding, a commitment from all involved countries, education, and improving the status of women are ways to fight the crisis, they claim. Kanabus is the project director for AVERT, an international HIV/AIDS agency. Fredriksson-Bass and Pembrey are writers.

As you read, consider the following questions:

1. What is the triple challenge faced by sub-Saharan Africa, according to the authors?

2. Between what ages are the vast majority of people living with HIV/AIDS in Africa, as the authors report?

3. What is the chance that an infected mother will pass HIV to her child without taking antiretroviral drugs, according to the authors?

Annabel Kanabus, Jenni Fredriksson-Bass, and Graham Pembrey, "HIV and AIDS in Africa," *The HIV & AIDS Epidemic in Africa*, West Sussex, UK: Avert.org, 2009. Copyright © AVERT. Reproduced by permission.

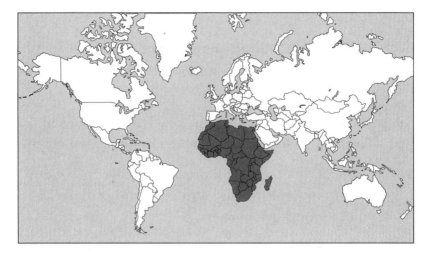

Sub-Saharan Africa is more heavily affected by HIV [human immunodeficiency virus] and AIDS [acquired immunodeficiency syndrome] than any other region of the world. An estimated 22 million people are living with HIV in the region—around two-thirds of the global total. In 2007 around 1.5 million people died from AIDS in sub-Saharan Africa and 1.9 million people became infected with HIV. Since the beginning of the epidemic more than eleven million children have been orphaned by AIDS, [according to the United Nations].

In the absence of massively expanded prevention, treatment and care efforts, it is expected that the AIDS death toll in sub-Saharan Africa will continue to rise. This means the impact of the AIDS epidemic on these societies will be felt most strongly in the course of the next ten years and beyond [2019 forward]. Its social and economic consequences are already widely felt, not only in the health sector but also in education, industry, agriculture, transport, human resources and the economy in general. The AIDS epidemic in sub-Saharan Africa threatens to devastate whole communities, rolling back decades of development progress.

Sub-Saharan Africa faces a triple challenge:

- Providing health care, antiretroviral treatment, and support to a growing population of people with HIV-related illnesses.

- Reducing the annual toll of new HIV infections by enabling individuals to protect themselves and others.

- Coping with the impact of over 20 million AIDS deaths on orphans and other survivors, communities, and national development.

In three southern African countries, the national adult HIV prevalence rate now exceeds 20%.

HIV/AIDS Statistics by Country

Both HIV prevalence rates and the numbers of people dying from AIDS vary greatly between African countries.

In Somalia and Senegal the HIV prevalence is under 1% of the adult population, whereas in Namibia, South Africa, Zambia and Zimbabwe around 15–20% of adults are infected with HIV. In three southern African countries, the national adult HIV prevalence rate now exceeds 20%. These countries are Botswana (23.9%), Lesotho (23.2%) and Swaziland (26.1%).

West Africa has been less affected by HIV and AIDS, but some countries are experiencing rising HIV prevalence rates. In Cameroon, HIV prevalence is now estimated at 5.1% and in Gabon it stands at 5.9%. In Nigeria, HIV prevalence is low (3.1%) compared to the rest of Africa. However, because of its large population (it is the most populous country in sub-Saharan Africa), this equates to around 2.6 million people living with HIV.

Adult HIV prevalence in East Africa exceeds 5% in Uganda, Kenya and Tanzania. [Editor's note: All statistics are from the United Nations.]

Overall, rates of new HIV infections in sub-Saharan Africa appear to have peaked in the late 1990s, and HIV prevalence seems to have declined slightly, although it remains at an extremely high level. . . .

Average life expectancy in sub-Saharan Africa is now 47 years, when it could have been 62 without AIDS.

The Impact of Aids on Africa

HIV and AIDS are having a widespread impact on many parts of African society. The points below describe some of the major effects of the AIDS epidemic. . . .

- *The effect on life expectancy.* In many countries of sub-Saharan Africa, AIDS is erasing decades of progress made in extending life expectancy. Millions of adults are dying from AIDS while they are still young, or in early middle age. Average life expectancy in sub-Saharan Africa is now 47 years, when it could have been 62 without AIDS.

- *The effect on households.* The effect of the AIDS epidemic on households can be very severe. Many families are losing their income earners. In other cases, people have to provide home-based care for sick relatives, reducing their capacity to earn money for their family. Many of those dying from AIDS have surviving partners who are themselves infected and in need of care. They leave behind orphans, grieving and struggling to survive without a parent's care.

- *The effect on health care.* In all affected countries, the epidemic is putting strain on the health sector. As the epidemic develops, the demand for care for those living with HIV rises, as does the number of health care workers affected.

- *The effect on schools.* Schools are heavily affected by AIDS. This [is] a major concern because schools can play a vital role in reducing the impact of the epidemic, through HIV education and support.

- *The effect on productivity.* The HIV and AIDS epidemic has dramatically affected labour, which in turn slows down economic activity and social progress. The vast majority of people living with HIV and AIDS in Africa are between the ages of 15 and 49—in the prime of their working lives. Employers, schools, factories and hospitals have to train other staff to replace those at the workplace who become too ill to work.

- *The effect on economic growth and development.* The HIV and AIDS epidemic has already significantly affected Africa's economic development, and in turn, has affected Africa's ability to cope with the epidemic.

HIV Prevention Strategies

A number of African countries have conducted large-scale HIV prevention initiatives in an effort to reduce the scale of their epidemics. Senegal, for example, responded early to the emergence of HIV with strong political and community leadership. It is impossible to predict how Senegal's epidemic would have progressed without intervention, but Senegal now has one of the lowest HIV prevalence rates in sub-Saharan Africa.

The situation in Uganda is similarly successful. HIV prevalence among pregnant women in Uganda fell from a high of around 30% in the early 1990s to around 10% in 2001; a change which is thought to be largely a result of intensive

HIV prevention campaigns. Declines in HIV prevalence have also been seen in Kenya, Zimbabwe and urban areas of Zambia and Burkina Faso.

However, not all African countries have had such successful HIV prevention campaigns. In South Africa, the government's failure to respond to the AIDS crisis has led to an unprecedented number of people living with HIV. An estimated 70,000 babies are born with HIV every year, reflecting significant failures in prevention of mother-to-child transmission initiatives.

Condoms play a key role in preventing HIV infection around the world. In sub-Saharan Africa, most countries have seen an increase in condom use in recent years. In studies carried out between 2001 and 2005, eight out of eleven countries in sub-Saharan Africa reported an increase in condom use.

An estimated 70,000 babies are born with HIV every year, reflecting significant failures in prevention of mother-to-child transmission initiatives.

The distribution of condoms to countries in sub-Saharan Africa has also increased: In 2004, the number of condoms provided to this region by donors was the equivalent of 10 for every man, compared to 4.6 for every man in 2001. In most countries, though, many more condoms are still needed. For instance, in Uganda between 120 and 150 million condoms are required annually, but less than 40 million were provided in 2005.

Relative to the enormity of the HIV/AIDS epidemic in Africa, providing condoms is cheap and cost effective. Even when condoms are available, though, there are still a number of social, cultural and practical factors that may prevent people from using them. In the context of stable partnerships where pregnancy is desired, or where it may be difficult for one partner to suddenly suggest condom use, this option may not be practical.

The provision of voluntary HIV counselling and testing (VCT) is an important part of any national prevention programme. It is widely recognized that individuals living with HIV who are aware of their status are less likely to transmit HIV infection to others, and are more likely to access treatment, care and support that can help them to stay healthy for longer. VCT also provides benefit for those who test negative, in that their behaviour may change as a result of the test.

The provision of VCT has become easier, cheaper and more effective as a result of the introduction of rapid HIV testing, which allows individuals to receive a test and the results in the same day. VCT could—and needs to be—made more widely available in most sub-Saharan African countries.

Mother-to-Child Transmission (MTCT)

Around 1.8 million children in sub-Saharan Africa were living with HIV at the end of 2007, representing around 90% of all children living with HIV worldwide. The vast majority of these children have been infected with HIV during pregnancy, childbirth or breast-feeding, as a result of their mothers being infected with HIV.

Without interventions, there is a 20–45% chance that an HIV-positive mother will pass infection on to her child. If a woman is supplied with antiretroviral drugs, however, this risk can be significantly reduced. Before these measures can be taken the mother must be aware of her HIV infection, so testing also plays a vital role in the prevention of MTCT.

Around 1.8 million children in sub-Saharan Africa were living with HIV at the end of 2007, representing around 90% of all children living with HIV worldwide.

In many developed countries, these steps have helped to virtually eliminate MTCT. Yet sub-Saharan Africa continues to be severely affected by the problem, due to a lack of drugs,

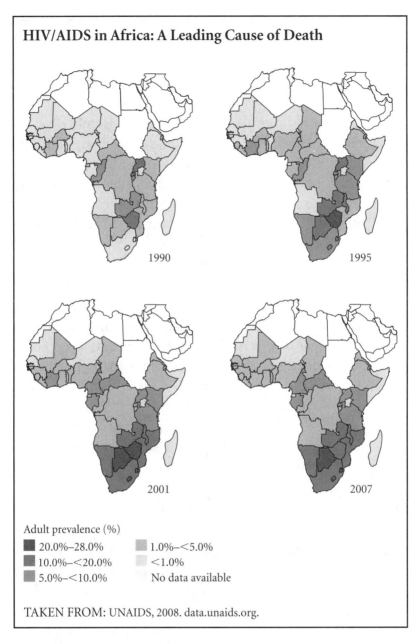

HIV/AIDS in Africa: A Leading Cause of Death

Adult prevalence (%)

- 20.0%–28.0%
- 10.0%–<20.0%
- 5.0%–<10.0%
- 1.0%–<5.0%
- <1.0%
- No data available

TAKEN FROM: UNAIDS, 2008. data.unaids.org.

services and information, and the shortage of testing facilities. In 2006, preventive drugs reached only 31% of HIV-infected pregnant women in Eastern and Southern Africa, and only 7% in West and Central Africa.

Given the scale of the MTCT crisis in Africa, it is remarkable that more is not being done (by both the international community and domestic governments) to prevent the rising numbers of children becoming infected with HIV, and dying from AIDS. . . .

Antiretroviral drugs (ARVs)—which significantly delay the progression of HIV to AIDS and allow people living with HIV to live relatively normal, healthy lives—have been available in richer parts of the world since around 1996. Distributing these drugs requires money, a well-structured health system and a sufficient supply of health care workers. The majority of developing countries are lacking in these areas and have struggled to cope with the increasing numbers of people requiring treatment.

For most Africans living with HIV, ARVs are still not available—fewer than one in three in need of treatment are receiving it [according to the World Health Organization (WHO)]. Millions are not even receiving treatment for opportunistic infections, which affect individuals whose immune systems have been weakened by HIV infection. These facts reflect the world's continuing failure, despite the progress of recent years, to mount a response that matches the scale and severity of the global AIDS epidemic. . . .

How to Prevent HIV/AIDS Deaths

One of the most important ways in which the situation in Africa can be improved is through increased funding for HIV/AIDS. More money would help to improve both prevention campaigns and the provision of treatment and care for those living with HIV. Developed countries have increased funding for the fight against AIDS in Africa in recent years, perhaps most significantly through the Global Fund. The Global Fund was started in 2001 to coordinate international funding and has since approved grants totalling US $7.2 billion to help fight AIDS, TB [tuberculosis] and malaria in 137 countries.

This funding is making a significant difference, but given the massive scale of the AIDS epidemic more money is still needed.

The US government has shown a commitment to fighting AIDS in Africa through the President's Emergency Plan For AIDS Relief (PEPFAR). Started in 2003, PEPFAR provides money to fight AIDS in numerous countries, including 15 focus countries, most of which are African. In fiscal year 2009, PEPFAR allocated almost US $6.5 billion for combating AIDS, TB and malaria. The US government is also the largest contributor to the Global Fund.

Among other things, organisations like PEPFAR and the Global Fund provide vital support to local and community groups that are working 'on the ground' to provide relief in Africa. These groups are directly helping people in need, and many rely on international funding in order to operate. Getting money from large, international donors to small, 'grassroots organisations' can present a number of difficulties though, as money is lost or delayed as it is passed down large funding chains.

African Countries Must Be Committed

More than money is needed if HIV prevention and treatment programmes are to be scaled up in Africa. In order to implement such programmes, a country's health, education and communication systems and infrastructures must be sufficiently developed. In some African countries these systems are already under strain and are at risk of collapsing as a result of AIDS. Money can also only be used efficiently if there are sufficient human resources available, but there is an acute shortage of trained personnel in many parts of Africa.

In many cases, African countries also need more commitment from their governments. There are promising signs that some governments are starting to respond and becoming more involved in the fight against AIDS, and this commitment needs to be sustained if the severe impact of Africa's AIDS epidemic is to be reduced.

HIV-related stigma and discrimination remains an enormous barrier to the fight against AIDS. Fear of discrimination often prevents people from getting tested, seeking treatment and admitting their HIV status publicly. Since laws and policies alone cannot reverse the stigma that surrounds HIV infection, AIDS education in Africa needs to be scaled up to combat the ignorance that causes people to discriminate. The fear and prejudice that lie at the core of HIV and AIDS discrimination need to be tackled at both community and national levels.

Women and Girls Must Be Helped

In many parts of Africa, as elsewhere in the world, the AIDS epidemic is aggravated by social and economic inequalities between men and women. Women and girls commonly face discrimination in terms of access to education, employment, credit, health care, land and inheritance. These factors can all put women in a position where they are particularly vulnerable to HIV infection. In sub-Saharan Africa, around 59% of those living with HIV are female.

In many African countries, sexual relationships are dominated by men, meaning that women cannot always practice safer sex even when they know the risks involved. Attempts are currently being made to develop a microbicide—a cream or gel that can be applied to the vagina, preventing HIV infection—which could be a significant breakthrough in protecting women against HIV. It is likely to be some time before a microbicide is ready for use, though, and even when it is, women will only use it if they have an awareness and understanding of HIV and AIDS. To promote this, a greater emphasis needs to be placed on educating women and girls about AIDS, and adapting education systems to their needs. In some Southern

African countries the rate of HIV among 23–24-year-old females is far higher than that of 15–17-year-old girls. This suggests prevention activities should target women at a young age and ensure they have the knowledge and skills to avoid HIV infection from when they become sexually active, [according to the United Nations Children's Fund (UNICEF)].

Scotland Experiences a Rise in Drug-Related Deaths

Tanya Thompson

In the following viewpoint, Tanya Thompson reports that drug deaths in the so-called "Trainspotting generation," people who began using intravenous drugs twenty to thirty years ago, are rising sharply in Scotland. The rates increased more for older drug users, she asserts. Social isolation and ill health from years of drug use were cited as reasons for the increase. According to Thompson, the Scottish Labour Party attacked the ruling Scottish National Party (SNP), saying they were "losing the battle against drugs." Thompson is the social affairs correspondent for the Scotsman.

As you read, consider the following questions:

1. According to statistics provided in the viewpoint, what was the percentage of increase in deaths among those aged 35–44?

2. According to Tanya Thompson, what percentage of drug deaths was among men?

3. What two drugs were most commonly cited as cause of death? How many deaths also included alcohol, according to the viewpoint?

Tanya Thompson, "Trainspotting Generation Pays the Price of Drugs," *The Scotsman*, August 13, 2009, p. 10. Copyright © 2009 The Scotsman Publications Ltd. Reproduced by permission.

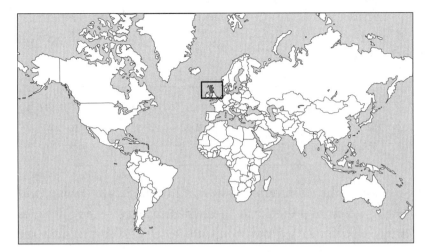

The human cost of long-term drug use was laid bare yesterday [August 12, 2009], as figures show Scotland's drug death toll has risen to record levels, with a sharp increase in deaths among older users.

And last night government ministers warned that drug deaths could continue to rise in the future, as the next generation of addicts faced the consequences of experimenting with drugs in their youth.

Health experts are blaming the "Trainspotting generation"[1]—those who began injecting heroin in the 1980s and 1990s—for the increased deaths.

A new report shows drug deaths have increased by more than a quarter in the past year, with the number of fatalities rising significantly among older people.

Drug-related deaths in Scotland have rocketed by more than 131 per cent over the past ten years, leading to calls for urgent action.

1. The "Trainspotting generation" is named for the influential 1996 Scottish film *Trainspotting*, directed by Danny Boyle. The film follows the lives of a group of young Scottish drug addicts.

Figures show the 35–44 age bracket made up 30 per cent of drug-related fatalities and 37 per cent were aged between 25 and 34 years old.

Drug-related deaths in Scotland have rocketed by more than 131 per cent over the past ten years, leading to calls for urgent action.

Last night, community safety minister Fergus Ewing said: "As a legacy of long-term drug misuse over recent decades, drug-related deaths may continue to rise over the next few years, especially among older men.

"It's a long-term problem with no single solution. That is why we must continue to take action to tackle this issue now and for the long term."

A Cause for Alarm

It is the rise in the number of deaths in the older age categories that is causing the greatest alarm for doctors of the National [Forum on] Drug-Related Deaths. . . . Deaths rose faster for 35–44-year-olds and for people aged 45 and over. Last year, deaths of those aged 35–44 increased 17 per cent to 174 on the previous year. Even more worrying, the number for those 45 and over rose 54 per cent last year to 97.

Experts said Scotland was dealing with a legacy reaching as far back as the late 1970s and 1980s, when many people began experimenting with drugs for the first time. Those injecting drugs such as heroin 20 years ago are now inheriting a range of serious health problems, including heart and respiratory illnesses, which, in some cases, are leading to premature death.

Drug charities said "social isolation" could be behind the deaths of older addicts.

Biba Brand, of Scottish Drugs Forum, said: "It is difficult to tell exactly why older drug users are increasingly featuring among the drug death statistics.

"However, many will have been using drugs—primarily heroin—for a long time.

"As a result, their physical health will have deteriorated and many will have become increasingly socially isolated over the years. This could make them more vulnerable to accidental or deliberate overdose."

The report, from the General Register Office for Scotland, revealed drugs killed 574 people in 2008, up from 455 the year before, and the number of deaths has more than doubled in a decade.

Heroin and morphine were responsible for the bulk of the deaths, with 80 per cent of the deaths among men.

Heroin remains a threat to public health, with figures showing heroin and morphine present in the body in 336 cases—59 per cent of deaths. Methadone was present in 181 cases—32 per cent, while cocaine, amphetamines and ecstasy were present in the body in 79, 12 and seven cases respectively.

The General Register Office for Scotland report said the long-term trend of drug deaths "appears to be steadily upwards". Throughout Scotland, there were wide variations, with the Greater Glasgow and Clyde NHS [National Health Service] Board area accounting for 34 per cent of the deaths, Lothian 16 per cent and Tayside 9 per cent.

The Scottish Government Takes Action

Mr. Ewing insisted yesterday that the Scottish government was trying to tackle the problem, citing a database launched this year [2009] to look at the circumstances behind each death. He said: "These figures demonstrate the real impact of drug misuse, which extends far beyond the individual drug user—it destroys lives."

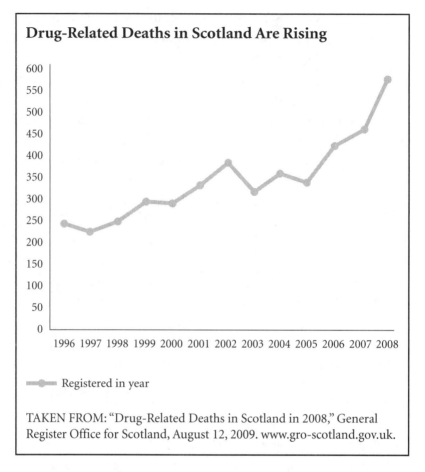

Drug-Related Deaths in Scotland Are Rising

Registered in year

TAKEN FROM: "Drug-Related Deaths in Scotland in 2008," General Register Office for Scotland, August 12, 2009. www.gro-scotland.gov.uk.

Marnie Hodge, development manager for social care agency Turning Point Scotland (TPS), said the increase in deaths might be the result of long-term drug misuse and it was crucial that addicts got the help they needed.

"TPS is working to ensure we provide a programme of interventions particularly designed for people who do not engage with support services and are, therefore, more exposed to the serious health risks, including the risk of overdose by the prolonged and persistent drug use."

Last year's [2008's] figures mark the third successive rise in drug-related deaths. Heroin or morphine was found in 336 bodies, with alcohol detected in 273 cases. Controversially, heroin substitute methadone was found in one-third of cases—calling into question the efficacy of the government's drug treatment policy.

Dr. Roy Robertson, chairman of the National [Forum on] Drug-Related Deaths . . . , described the methadone figure as "alarming", but defended the use of the drug for those addicted to heroin.

Last year's [2008's] figures mark the third successive rise in drug-related deaths.

He said: "Every country that has drug use problems debates this constantly and incessantly, about the relative value of methadone against the risks. We know that methadone, by and large, is a successful treatment."

Labour [political party] claimed the SNP [Scottish Nationalist Party] were losing the battle against drugs, accusing them of failing to deliver. Justice spokeswoman Cathy Jamieson said: "The rise in the number of drug-related deaths is extremely worrying, and we need action from ministers to reverse the trend."

She said: "The SNP promised a 20 per cent increase in funding for drugs treatment in their manifesto, but, like so many other promises, they have failed to deliver it. Ministers have also cut budgets to local agencies supporting drug addicts."

Conservative leader Annabel Goldie said the figures reflected "a wasted decade".

Russia Is Facing a Death Crisis

Nicholas Eberstadt

In the following viewpoint, Nicholas Eberstadt reports that Russia suffers from a slide in population, brought about by a sharply falling fertility rate, devaluation of the status of children, a serious HIV/AIDS epidemic, the highest rate of cardiovascular disease in the world, and a pattern of death from injury and violence. Alcohol abuse is also prevalent, the author asserts, and contributes to deaths in all areas. He warns that the rate of depopulation carries "potentially disastrous implications." Eberstadt holds the Henry Wendt Chair in Political Economy at the American Enterprise Institute (AEI) and is senior advisor to the National Bureau of Asian Research (NBR).

As you read, consider the following questions:

1. What does the United Nations Population Division project that Russia's population will be in the year 2025?

2. How do the rates of a woman's risk of death in childbirth in Russia compare to those in Germany and Switzerland, according to WHO estimates from 2005?

3. According to the WHO, how many new tuberculosis (TB) infections per year is Russia facing? What percentage of this number is extreme drug-resistant tuberculosis?

Nicholas Eberstadt, "Drunken Nation: Russia's Depopulation Bomb," *World Affairs*, Spring 2009. Copyright © 2009 by Helen Dwight Reid Educational Foundation. Reproduced with permission of the Helen Dwight Reid Educational Foundation, published by Heldref Publications, 1319 18th Street, NW, Washington, DC 20036-1802.

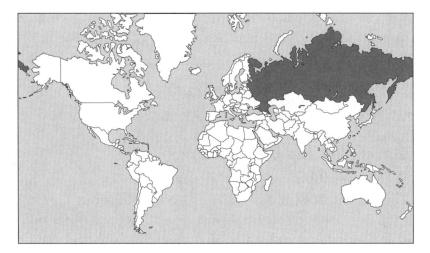

A specter is haunting Russia today. It is not the specter of communism—that ghost has been chained in the attic of the past—but rather of depopulation—a relentless, unremitting, and perhaps unstoppable depopulation. The mass deaths associated with the Communist era may be history, but another sort of mass death may have only just begun, as Russians practice what amounts to an ethnic self-cleansing.

Since 1992, Russia's human numbers have been progressively dwindling. This slow motion process now taking place in the country carries with it grim and potentially disastrous implications that threaten to recast the contours of life and society in Russia, to diminish the prospects for Russian economic development, and to affect Russia's potential influence on the world stage in the years ahead.

Russia has faced this problem at other times during the last century. The first bout of depopulation lasted from 1917 to 1923, and was caused by the upheavals that transformed the Russian Empire into the Soviet Union. The next drop took place between 1933 and 1934, when the country's population fell by nearly 2 million—or almost 2 percent—as a result of [Joseph] Stalin's war against the "kulaks" in his forced collectivization of Soviet agriculture. And then, between 1941 and

1946, Russia's population plummeted by more than 13 million through the cataclysms and catastrophes of World War II.

Since 1992, Russia's human numbers have been progressively dwindling.

Current Russian Depopulation Is Not Abating

The current Russian depopulation—which began in 1992 and shows no signs of abating—was, like the previous episodes, also precipitated by events of momentous political significance: the final dissolution of the Soviet Union and the end of Communist Party rule. But it differs in three important respects. First, it is by far the longest period of population decline in modern Russian history, having persisted for over twice as long as the decline that followed the Bolshevik Revolution, and well over three times as long as the terrifying depopulation Russia experienced during and immediately after World War II.

Second, unlike all the previous depopulations in Russia, this one has been taking place under what are, within the Russian context, basically orderly social and political circumstances. Terror and war are not the engines for the depopulation Russia is experiencing today, as they have been in the past.

And finally, whereas Russia's previous depopulations resulted from wild and terrible social paroxysms, they were also clearly temporary in nature. The current crisis, on the other hand, is proceeding gradually and routinely, and thus it is impossible to predict when, or whether, it will finally come to an end.

A comparison dramatizes what is happening in Russia. Between 1976 and 1991, the last sixteen years of Soviet power, the country recorded 36 million births. In the sixteen post-

Communist years of 1992–2007, there were just 22.3 million, a drop in childbearing of nearly 40 percent from one era to the next. On the other side of the life cycle, a total of 24.6 million deaths were recorded between 1976 and 1991, while in the first sixteen years of the post-Communist period the Russian Federation tallied 34.7 million deaths, a rise of just over 40 percent. The symmetry is striking: In the last sixteen years of the Communist era, births exceeded deaths in Russia by 11.4 million; in the first sixteen years of the post-Soviet era, deaths exceeded births by 12.4 million. . . .

Predicting Russia's Future

So where, given these daunting facts, is the Russian Federation headed demographically in the years and decades ahead? Two of the world's leading demographic institutions—the United Nations Population Division (UNPD) and the U.S. Bureau of the Census—have tried to answer this question by a series of projections based upon what their analysts believe to be plausible assumptions about Russia's future fertility, mortality, and migration patterns.

Both organizations' projections trace a continuing downward course for the Russian Federation's population over the generation ahead. As of mid-year 2005, Russia's estimated population was around 143 million. UNPD projections for the year 2025 range from a high of about 136 million to a low of about 121 million; for the year 2030, they range from 133 million to 115 million. The Census Bureau's projections for the Russian Federation's population in 2025 and 2030 are 128 million and 124 million, respectively.

If these projections turn out to be relatively accurate—admittedly, a big "if" for any long-range demographic projection—the Russian Federation will have experienced over thirty years of continuous demographic decline by 2025, and the better part of four decades of depopulation by 2030. Russia's population would then have dropped by about 20 million between 1990 and 2025, and Russia would have fallen from the world's sixth to the twelfth most populous country. In relative terms, that would amount to almost as dramatic a demographic drop as the one Russia suffered during World War II [1939–1945]. In absolute terms, it would actually be somewhat greater in magnitude. . . .

Russian Fertility Rates

In the late 1980s, near the end of the Communist era, there were just a handful of European countries (most of them under Communist rule) with higher fertility rates than Russia's. By 2005, the last year for which authoritative data is available, there were only a few European societies (perhaps ironically, most of them ex-Communist) with lower rates.

What accounts for the Russian Federation's low levels of fertility? Some observers point to poor health conditions. And indeed, as we will see, Russia's overall health situation today is truly woeful. This is especially true of its reproductive health.

A consortium headed by the World Health Organization [WHO] estimated that for 2005 a woman's risk of death in childbirth in Russia was over six times higher than in Germany or Switzerland. Moreover, mortality levels for women in their twenties (the decade in which childbearing is concentrated in contemporary Russia) have been rising, not falling, in recent decades.

But Russia's low fertility patterns are not due to any extraordinary inability of Russian women to conceive, but rather to the strong and growing tendency among childbearing women to have no more than two children—and perhaps increasingly not more than one. The new evident limits on family size in Russia, in turn, suggest a sea change in the country's norms concerning family formation.

In 1980, fewer than one Russian newborn in nine was reportedly born out of wedlock. By 2005, the country's illegitimacy ratio was approaching 30 percent—almost tripling in just twenty years. Marriage is not only less common in Russia today than in the recent past; it is also markedly less stable. In 2005, the total number of marriages celebrated in Russia was down by nearly one-fourth from 1980 (a fairly typical [Soviet Union leader Leonid] Brezhnev-period year for marriages). On the other hand, the total number of divorces recognized in Russia has been on an erratic rise over the past generation, from under 400 divorces per 1,000 marriages in 1980 to a peak of over 800 in 2002.

In 1990, the end of the [former president Mikhail] Gorbachev era, marriage was still the norm, and while divorce was very common, a distinct majority of Russian Federation women (60 percent) could expect to have entered into a first marriage and still remain in that marriage by age 50. A few years later, in 1996, the picture was already radically different: Barely a third of Russia's women (34 percent) were getting married and staying in that same marriage until age 50.

Since the end of the Soviet era, young women in Russia are opting for cohabitation before and, to a striking extent, instead of marriage. In the early 1980s, about 15 percent of women had been in consensual unions by age 25; twenty years later, the proportion was 45 percent. Many fewer of those once-cohabiting young women, moreover, seem to be moving into marital unions nowadays. Whereas roughly a generation earlier, fully half of cohabiters were married within a year, today less than a third are. . . .

Ramifications of Fertility Decline Plus Mortality Gains

There are many ramifications of the dramatic decline in population in Russia, but three in particular bear heavily on the country's prospective development and national security.

First, when Western European nations reached the level of 30 percent illegitimate births that Russia has now attained, their levels of per capita output were all dramatically higher—

three times higher in France, Austria, and Britain, and higher than that in countries such as Germany, Ireland, and the Netherlands. This means that Russia's mothers and their children will be afforded far fewer of the social protections that their counterparts could count on in Western Europe's more generous welfare states.

In post-Communist Russia, there are unambiguous indications of a worsening of social well-being for a significant proportion of the country's children—in effect, a disinvestment in children.

A second and related point pertains to "investment" in children. According to prevailing tenets of Western economic thought, a decline in fertility—to the extent that it occurs under conditions of orderly progress, and as a consequence of parental volition—should mean a better material environment for newborns and children because a shift to smaller desired family size, all else being equal, signifies an increase in parents' expected commitments to each child's education, nutrition, health care, and the like.

Yet in post-Communist Russia, there are unambiguous indications of a worsening of social well-being for a significant proportion of the country's children—in effect, a disinvestment in children in the face of a pronounced downward shift in national fertility patterns. . . .

The 1960s and 1970s witnessed an increase in mortality rates for key elements of the Soviet population. But Russia's health patterns did not correct course with the collapse of the USSR [Union of Soviet Socialist Republics], as many experts assumed they would. In fact, in the first decade and a half of its post-Communist history the country's health conditions actually became worse. Life expectancy in the Russian Federation is actually lower today than it was a half century ago in the late 1950s. In fact, the country has pioneered a unique

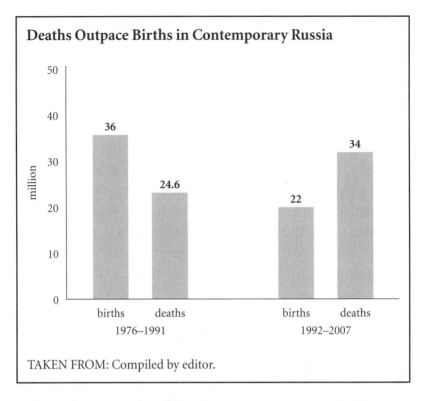

Deaths Outpace Births in Contemporary Russia

TAKEN FROM: Compiled by editor.

new profile of mass debilitation and foreshortened life previously unknown in all of human history.

Like the urbanized and literate societies in Western Europe, North America, and elsewhere, the overwhelming majority of deaths in Russia today accrue from chronic rather than infectious diseases: heart disease, cancers, strokes, and the like. But in the rest of the developed world, death rates from these chronic diseases are low, relatively stable, and declining regularly over time. In the Russian Federation, by contrast, overall mortality levels are high, manifestly unstable, and rising.

Life Expectancy Signals a Dangerous Pattern

The single clearest and most comprehensible summary measure of a population's mortality prospects is its estimated expectation of life at birth. Russia's trends in the late 1950s and early 1960s were rising briskly. In the five years between 1959 and 1964, for instance, life expectancy increased by more than two years. But then, inexplicably, overall health progress in Russia came to a sudden and spectacular halt. Over that 18-year period that roughly coincides with the Brezhnev era, Russia's life expectancy not only stagnated, but actually fell by about a year and a half.

These losses were recovered during the Gorbachev period, but even at its pinnacle in 1986 and 1987, overall life expectancy for Russia was only marginally higher than it had been in 1964, never actually managing to cross the symbolic 70-year threshold. With the end of communism, moreover, life expectancy went into erratic decline, plummeting a frightful four years between 1992 and 1994, recovering somewhat through 1998, but then again spiraling downward. In 2006—the most recent year for which we have such data—overall Russian life expectancy at birth was over three years lower than it had been in 1964.

The situation for Russian males has been particularly woeful. In the immediate postwar era, life expectancy for men was somewhat lower than in other developed countries—but this differential might partly be attributed to the special hardships of World War II and the evils of Stalinism. By the early 1960s, the male life expectancy gap between Russia and the more developed regions narrowed somewhat—but then life expectancy for Russian men entered into a prolonged and agonizing decline, while continued improvements characterized most of the rest of the world. By 2005, male life expectancy at birth was fully fifteen years lower in the Russian Federation than in Western Europe. It was also five years below the global average for male life expectancy, and three years below the average for the less developed regions (whose levels it had exceeded, in the early 1950s, by fully two decades). Put another way, male life expectancy in 2006 was about two and a half years lower under [Russian president Vladimir] Putin than it had been in 1959, under [Soviet Cold War leader Nikita] Khrushchev.

According to the U.S. Census Bureau International Data Base for 2007, Russia ranked 164 out of 226 globally in overall life expectancy. Russia is below Bolivia, South America's poorest (and least healthy) country and lower than Iraq and India, but somewhat higher than Pakistan. For females, the Russian Federation life expectancy will not be as high as in Nicaragua, Morocco, or Egypt. For males, it will be in the same league as that of Cambodia, Ghana, and Eritrea.

By 2005, male life expectancy at birth was fully fifteen years lower in the Russian Federation than in Western Europe.

In the face of today's exceptionally elevated mortality levels for Russia's young adults, it is no wonder that an unspecified proportion of the country's would-be mothers and fathers respond by opting for fewer offspring than they would otherwise desire. To a degree not generally appreciated, Russia's current fertility crisis is a consequence of its mortality crisis.

How did Russia's mortality level, which was nearly 38 percent higher than Western Europe's in 1980, skyrocket to an astonishing 135 percent higher in 2006? What role did communicable and infectious disease play in this fateful health regression and mortality deterioration?

Disease and Violence in Russia

By any reading, the situation in Russia today sounds awful. The Russian Federation is afflicted with a serious HIV [human immunodeficiency virus]/AIDS [acquired immunodeficiency syndrome] epidemic; according to UNAIDS [Joint United Nations Programme on HIV/AIDS], as of 2008 somewhere around 1 million Russians were living with the virus. (Russia's HIV nexus appears to be closely associated with a burgeoning phenomenon of local drug use, with sex trafficking and other forms of prostitution or "commercial sex," and with other practices and mores relating to extramarital sex.) Russia also faces a related and evidently growing burden of tuberculosis [TB]. As of 2008, according to World Health Organization [WHO] estimates, Russia was experiencing about 150,000 new TB infections a year. To make matters worse, almost half of Russia's treated tubercular cases over the past decade have been the variant known as extreme drug-resistant tuberculosis (XDR-TB).

Yet, dismaying as these statistics are, the picture looks even worse when we consider cardiovascular disease (CVD) mortality trends.

No literate and urban society in the modern world faces a risk of deaths from injuries comparable to the one that Russia experiences.

By the late 1960s, the epidemic upsurge of CVD mortality in Western industrial societies that immediately followed World War II had peaked. From the mid-1970s onward, age-standardized death rates from diseases of the circulatory system steadily declined in Western Europe. In Russia, by stark contrast, CVD mortality in 1980 was well over 50 percent higher than it had been in "old" EU [European Union] states as of 1970, and the Russian population may well have been suffering the very highest incidence of mortality from diseases of the circulatory system that had ever been visited on a national population in the entire course of human history.

Over the subsequent decades, unfortunately, the level of CVD mortality in the Russian Federation veered even further upward. By 2006, Russia's CVD mortality rate, standardizing for population structure, was an almost unbelievable 3.8 times higher than the population-weighted level reported for Western Europe.

Scarcely less alarming was Russia's mortality rate from "external causes"—noncommunicable deaths from injuries of various origins. The tale here is broadly similar to the story of CVD: impossibly high levels of death in a society that otherwise does not exhibit signs of backwardness.

In Western Europe, age-standardized mortality from injury and poisoning, as tabulated by the World Health Organization, fell by almost half between 1970 and 2006. In Russia, on the other hand, deaths from injuries and poisoning, which had been 2.5 times higher than in Western Europe in 1980, were up to 5.3 times higher as of 2006.

A broadly negative relationship was evident between mortality from injuries and per capita income. In other Western countries in 2002, an increase of 10 percent in per capita GDP [gross domestic product] was associated with a drop of about 2 points in injury deaths per 100,000 population. Yet Russia's toll of deaths is nearly three times higher than would be predicted by its GDP. No literate and urban society in the modern world faces a risk of deaths from injuries comparable to the one that Russia experiences.

Russia's patterns of death from injury and violence (by whatever provenance) are so extreme and brutal that they invite comparison only with the most tormented spots on the face of the planet today. The five places estimated to be roughly in the same league as Russia as of 2002 were Angola, Burundi, Congo, Liberia, and Sierra Leone. To go by its level of mortality injury alone, Russia looks not like an emerging middle-income market economy at peace, but rather like an impoverished sub-Saharan conflict or post-conflict society.

Alcohol Abuse Leads to Death

Taken together, then, deaths from cardiovascular disease and from injuries and poisoning have evidently been the main drivers of modern Russia's strange upsurge in premature mortality and its broad, prolonged retrogression in public health conditions. One final factor that is intimately associated with both of these causes of mortality is alcohol abuse.

Unlike drinking patterns prevalent in, say, Mediterranean regions—where wine is regarded as an elixir for enhancing conversation over meals and other social gatherings, and where public drunkenness carries an embarrassing stigma—mind-numbing, stupefying binge drinking of hard spirits is an accepted norm in Russia and greatly increases the danger of fatal injury through falls, traffic accidents, violent confrontations, homicide, suicide, and so on. Further, extreme binge drinking (especially of hard spirits) is associated with stress on the cardiovascular system and heightened risk of CVD mortality.

How many Russians are actually drinkers, and how heavily do they actually drink? Officially, Russia classifies some 7 million out of roughly 120 million persons over 15 years of age, or roughly 6 percent of its adult population, as heavy drinkers. But the numbers are surely higher than this. According to data compiled by the World Health Organization, as of 2003 Russia was Europe's heaviest per capita spirits consumer; its reported hard liquor consumption was over four times as high as Portugal's, three times that of Germany or Spain, and over two and a half times higher than that of France.

Yet even these numbers may substantially understate hard spirit use in Russia, since the WHO figures follow only the retail sale of hard liquor. But *samogon*—home-brew, or "moonshine"—is, according to some Russian researchers, a huge component of the country's overall intake. Professor Alexander Nemstov, perhaps Russia's leading specialist in this area, argues that Russia's adult population—women as well as men—puts down the equivalent of a bottle of vodka per week.

From the epidemiological standpoint, local-level studies have offered fairly chilling proof that alcohol is a direct factor in premature mortality. One forensic investigation of blood alcohol content by a medical examiner's office in a city in the Urals, for example, indicated that over 40 percent of the younger male decedents evaluated had probably been alcohol-impaired or severely intoxicated at the time of death—including one-quarter of the deaths from heart disease and over half of those from accidents or injuries. But medical and epidemiological studies have also demonstrated that, in addition to its many deaths from consumption of ordinary alcohol, Russia also suffers a grisly toll from alcohol poisoning, as the country's drinkers, in their desperate quest for intoxication, down not only sometimes severely impure *samogon*, but also perfumes, alcohol-based medicines, cleaning solutions, and other deadly liquids. Death rates from such alcohol poisoning appear to be at least one hundred times higher in Russia than the United States—this despite the fact that the retail price in Russia today is lower for a liter of vodka than a liter of milk. . . .

Russia's Future Is in Jeopardy

In the modern era, population decline itself need not be a cause for acute economic alarm. Italy, Germany, and Japan are among the societies where signs of incipient population decline are being registered nowadays: All of these are affluent countries, and all can anticipate continuing improvements in their respective levels of prosperity (albeit at a slower tempo than some might prefer). Depopulation with Russian characteristics—population decline powered by an explosive upsurge of illness and mortality—is altogether more forbidding in its economic implications, not only forcing down popular well-being today, but also placing unforgiving constraints on economic productivity and growth for tomorrow.

As we have already seen, it is Russia's death crisis that accounts for the entirety of the country's population decline over the past decade and a half. The upsurge of illness and mortality, furthermore, has been disproportionately concentrated among men and women of working age—meaning that Russia's labor force has been shrinking more rapidly than the population overall.

Health is a critical and central element in the complex quantity that economists have termed "human capital." In the contemporary international economy, one additional year of life expectancy at birth is associated with an increase in per capita output of about 8 percent. A decade of lost life expectancy improvement would correspond to the loss of a doubling of per capita income. By this standard, Russia's economic as well as its demographic future is in jeopardy.

In Uganda, Ritual Killings Are on the Rise

New Vision

In the following viewpoint, New Vision, Uganda's leading news-paper, reports on the problem of increasing numbers of ritual murders. Some Ugandans and other Africans believe that by killing another human being in a sacrifice, they can change their luck and improve their financial and social status. The economy of Uganda has suffered with the worldwide economic crisis, says New Vision, and many are seeking employment or money as a result. Desperate people are resorting to ritual murders, especially of albinos, in the hopes of better lives for themselves.

As you read, consider the following questions:

1. How much money flowed into Uganda in 2008, according to the viewpoint?
2. What happened to Vumilia Makoye, according to the viewpoint?
3. What is the remedy to ritual murder, according to *New Vision*?

Last week [in February 2009], Kampala Police rounded up several suspects linked to the ritual killing of a woman in the city suburb of Bwaise.

Before he died in police custody, one of the suspects, Musa Bogere, apparently admitted killing the woman with two oth-

New Vision, "Uganda: Ritual Killing Cannot Make Anyone Richer," February 17, 2009. Reproduced by permission.

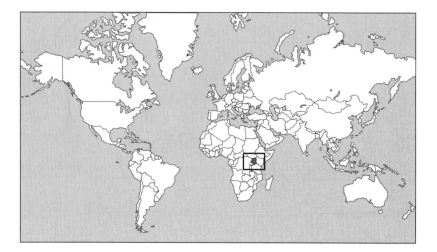

ers, chopping off her limbs and private parts, before dumping the body in a latrine. The killing was a special request from the two customers who wanted to get employment.

Ritual Killings Are Tied to Economic Good Luck

In Swaziland, Tanzania, Ghana and Nigeria, ritual killings are tied to fortune, the participants hoping to change things in their favour. They could win an election or get that beautiful car. But more recently, simply get that job to earn a living.

While there is a tendency to blame animistic beliefs that encourage animal and human sacrifice behind these killings, the link to poverty cannot be ignored. More specifically, the economic crisis gripping the world, threatening to throw many out of work in North America, China, Japan, Europe and Asia has come to Africa. In these killings, one senses desperation, doing anything and everything in a rapidly dwindling economy where getting a job is considered good luck.

For a while, many never imagined that the global economic crisis could touch Africa. The main argument was that the underdeveloped economies of most African countries insulated them from the global economic turmoil.

African countries, the argument went, continue to rely mostly on farming and natural resources. As such, African economies lacked the sophistication that developed economies have such as a highly sensitive stock exchange, a robust banking system that provides loans to the consumer and a highly discriminating consumer that decides what to buy or not to buy. In the developing world, one has to first accumulate money before embarking piecemeal into a project like building a permanent home.

The World's Fortunes Are Africa's Fortunes

However, it is naïve to think that the current global economic crisis is not going to touch a person in Lomé, Ouagadougou, Windhoek, Antananarivo or Kampala. That is because developing economies are inextricably linked to the developed world. For instance, the annual remittances from abroad have in the past years boosted many African economies.

Ghanaians living abroad sent home $8b [billion] last year [2008], almost quadrupled what the domestic economy made. President Yoweri Museveni is on record for praising the importance of funds sent by Ugandans living overseas. More than $1b flowed into the country from abroad last year.

Beliefs persist among the urban poor whose animists' beliefs mix with urban tales to produce a cocktail of deadly plots to kill humans for riches.

All this is coming to an end as investment funds from abroad dry up, tourism drops as tourists choose to stay close to home to weather the downturn in the economy, and remittances from abroad decline due to rising unemployment for many Africans living abroad. As funds drop, so will economic fortunes of countries that have to depend on these sources of much-needed foreign money.

The impact in the marginally urban poor in Africa has been catastrophic with unemployment running as high as 25% in some countries. Some of the unemployed poor in developing countries have come to think in apocalyptic terms. *I am suffering because the world must be ending, and desperate times call for desperate measures. If killing another human being will greatly improve my chances of survival, so be it.*

This, of course, is pure nonsense—the world is not ending and killing another person does not make anyone better off or rich. It makes one a sinister murderer who should be dealt with by the law. Still, the beliefs persist among the urban poor whose animists' beliefs mix with urban tales to produce a cocktail of deadly plots to kill humans for riches.

Some fairly rich urban clients also likely believe that their businesses will flourish as a result of human ritual sacrifices.

Albinos Are the Target of Ritual Slayings

Unfortunately, these erroneous beliefs continue to spread over continental Africa. In the dying days of 2008 last year, a seven-year-old Kenyan albino named Greenstone Njoroge was murdered as he played with other children. In the wake of Njoroge's brutal slaying, the [Albino] Association of Kenya . . . called a press conference at which it strongly refuted the notion that killing an albino would make one rich. The association called on the government of Kenya to protect albinos in that country.

In Tanzania, for the past several months, albinos have been targeted by fetish practitioners who believe that using the rare albino body parts in ritual ceremonies would bring them fortune. Reports of daring attacks on albinos have included stories of body parts hacked off by the attackers, leaving the victims to bleed to death. In May 2008, a 17-year-old albino girl named Vumilia Makoye was eating dinner with her family in western Tanzania, when two men wielding long knives burst into the hut. Vumilia's mother tried to save her

---

Ritual Killings in Liberia

Locally called "Gboyo"—the practice of killing people so that their body parts can be extracted and offered as sacrifices to bring power, wealth and success—it is an ancient practice in Liberia that Liberian elites have not worked to deal with as part of its development process, making it grow to such an extent that on 29 June 2005, prior to Liberia's current democratic dispensation, its interim leader Gyude Bryant "warned any aspiring presidential candidates tempted to boost their chances by carrying out human sacrifices that they will be executed if caught. . . . If you think you can take somebody's life in order to be president, or the speaker (of parliament) or a senator, without anything being done to you, then you are fooling yourself."

Kofi Akosah-Sarpong,
"Liberia: Rampant Ritual Killings or Gboyo,"
Patriotic Vanguard, *August 8, 2007.*

---

daughter, but the men overpowered her, hacked off Vumilia's legs and disappeared with them, leaving her to bleed to death.

Vumilia's death will not be the last one, especially as the full force of the world economic crisis hits Africa. Rather than treating these as isolated cases, African governments, especially countries like Uganda and Tanzania, where the practice of ritual sacrifices has taken root need to do more than simply stand and look in disgust.

Governments must not only protect the vulnerable, but mount open education of the masses who believe in these dark rituals. There is a need to let people understand that your best chance of getting a job does not lie with killing an albino or chopping off the head of your neighbour's child, but in getting better education, and learning a marketable skill.

Of course, the urgent remedy is job creation that enables people to get decent wages.

In Ireland, Suicides Among Youth Are Increasing

Kevin Malone

Kevin Malone, a professor of psychiatry at University College Dublin and St. Vincent's University Hospital, decries the rate of Irish youth suicide in the following viewpoint. He suggests that the deaths may be a result of cluster influences, with one suicide leading to depression and suicide among the mourners. He notes that many support groups have sprung up around Ireland and that the government is taking action. He concludes that not enough is being done to safeguard Irish youth.

As you read, consider the following questions:

1. According to Kevin Malone, what are four things that contribute to the risk of a subsequent suicide loss in a community?
2. What is the rate of suicidal thoughts for adolescents in Spain, according to Malone?
3. As the author reports, how much per capita does Ireland spend on suicide prevention?

How many more tragedies of young lives lost to suicide do we need to witness in Ireland before we as a society can shout 'stop!' and 'enough!' with a sufficiently united voice of compassion and determination to make the necessary difference to reduce suicide deaths in our communities?

Kevin Malone, "Why Are Our Youngsters Killing Themselves at a Rate of One a Day?" *The Daily Mail*, June 20, 2007. Copyright © 2007 Solo Syndication Limited. Reproduced by permission of the author.

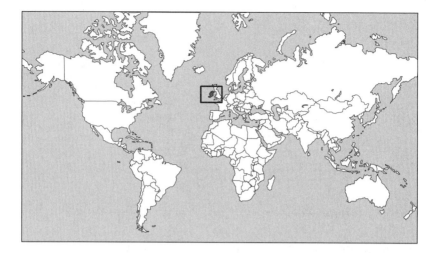

To a large extent we remain in a knowledge vacuum, or to put it more bluntly, in a state of complete ignorance about youth suicide in our society.

Does one suicide affect another, and if so, by which mechanisms?

Suicide Clusters

Undoubtedly, clusters of suicide are occurring in Ireland, but until now we have no way of systematically identifying whether this is the case or not.

Some external international experts are suggesting that perhaps suicide in Ireland is one rolling cluster, a kind of gradually growing domino effect, where in some way one suicide death possibly influences another potential suicide deaths, and that young men are particularly vulnerable to this effect.

Ireland is a nation made up of multiple small and somewhat closed communities, and a death, especially a sudden loss through suicide, has extra profound vibrations through the community.

Dealing with grief and loss is one of life's great challenges for humanity. We are no different in Ireland, and young people are prone to overidentifying with the loss of a peer or colleague.

With advances in life expectancy, young people have much less exposure to bereavement, and a death by suicide may be their first personal experience of loss. Appropriate mourning rituals as part of coping with the loss may be absent, and glorification, normalisation and idealisation may contribute to the risk of a subsequent affected suicide loss in the same community.

Clearly, within a framework of grief and loss, it is too simplistic to call it a 'copycat event'. An underlying stigma-effect can contribute to a sense of isolation amongst bereaved families who remain at increased risk.

A National Survey of Suicide in Ireland

We have recently commenced [the *Suicide in Ireland Survey*], which is focussing on learning about the lives lost to suicide over the past three years [since 2004] through interviewing family and friends of the suicide deaths. It is partially funded by the State, but largely through charitable donations, especially from the charity Turn the Tide of Suicide.

Some of the results of this study will for the first time be able to examine the connectivity between suicide deaths, and the possible influences that suicide deaths have on each other.

Thus we will be able to identify factors associated with clusters of suicide if they appear in our analyses.

Early evidence suggests the existence of multiple clusters, that younger age groups are particularly susceptible (not exclusively boys), and that communication between peers about possible suicide had occurred in most cases within a month prior to the death by suicide.

This obviously leaves enormous feelings of guilt, which complicate the bereavement process in those 'left behind' as they see it. If these findings continue through the whole study, it raises the question of how we are going to respond to young people who have knowledge about a suicidal friend (sometimes they are sworn to secrecy), to allow them to get help for their

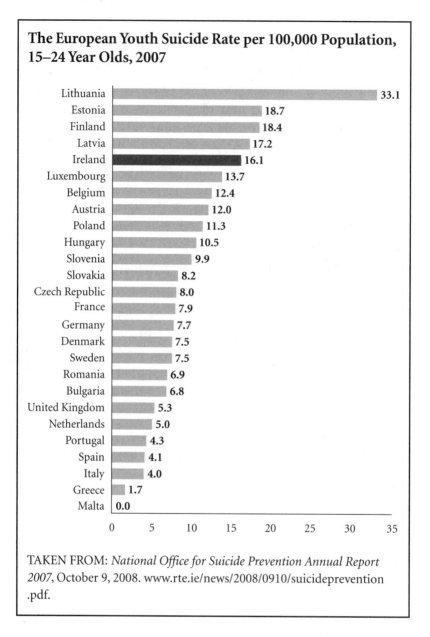

The European Youth Suicide Rate per 100,000 Population, 15–24 Year Olds, 2007

Country	Rate
Lithuania	33.1
Estonia	18.7
Finland	18.4
Latvia	17.2
Ireland	16.1
Luxembourg	13.7
Belgium	12.4
Austria	12.0
Poland	11.3
Hungary	10.5
Slovenia	9.9
Slovakia	8.2
Czech Republic	8.0
France	7.9
Germany	7.7
Denmark	7.5
Sweden	7.5
Romania	6.9
Bulgaria	6.8
United Kingdom	5.3
Netherlands	5.0
Portugal	4.3
Spain	4.1
Italy	4.0
Greece	1.7
Malta	0.0

TAKEN FROM: *National Office for Suicide Prevention Annual Report 2007*, October 9, 2008. www.rte.ie/news/2008/0910/suicideprevention .pdf.

young peer in difficulty. Suicide pacts are thankfully extremely rare, but are extremely worrying and tragic when they occur. Only through focused research will we learn more about this phenomenon.

Depression Remains Unrecognized

There is substantial evidence that we are failing to recognise depressive symptoms in our adolescents, and failing to respond or to provide services for response when these symptoms are finally recognised.

Teenagers won't call their feelings 'depression' but instead will identify unexplained bouts of 'sadness', 'tiredness' and sometimes 'anxiety and irritability'.

Oversleeping, social withdrawal and a loss of interest in activities (schoolwork or recreational), and of course an increased tendency to take alcohol, often as a form of self-medication, are also symptoms commonly associated with 'entering the red zone' in relation to risk of suicidal acts including suicide.

Almost 20 per cent of Irish adolescents surveyed recently [in 2007] had experienced some suicidal thoughts in the previous 12 months.

Engagement and open communication are extremely necessary. And bearing in mind that their friends will know about your son or daughter, brother or sister's mood dips before you will, it is valuable as a parent to get to know your kids' friends, so they feel comfortable engaging with you, and possibly turning to you for help for your loved one in a time of need.

We have to wonder why almost 20 per cent of Irish adolescents surveyed recently [in 2007] had experienced some suicidal thoughts in the previous 12 months. The figure for Spanish adolescents is between 1–2 per cent. We have let this problem quietly fester, choosing largely to turn a blind eye to the rising body count of lives lost to suicide. There are eight to ten suicide deaths per week in Ireland currently, and 50 per cent of these deaths are in those under 25.

Between 2003 and 2006 inclusive, there have been over 2,000 lives lost in Ireland, 1,000 of these under 25 years old, and there have been more lives lost to suicide in Ireland in the past five years than were lost through the violence of the previous 30 years of the Troubles [a period of ethnic and political violence in Ireland lasting from the 1960s through the 1990s].

Whilst increase in alcohol consumption among young people is a potential factor, less than 50 per cent of the young suicide deaths we have examined so far in our research project were associated with alcohol excess.

Supporting the Battle Against Teen Suicide

The response from communities has been one of enormous concern, with support groups springing up all over the country. These support activities at another level are energy-sapping and difficult to sustain, and funding is a continuing issue. The response from 'officialdom' has been lukewarm.

Despite the calculation that suicide in Ireland costs almost €900 million [euros] [about 14 million USD] a year, the government is funding a national suicide prevention strategy that equates to 50c [about 75¢ USD] per capita in Ireland compared with €2 [euros] [about 3.50 USD] per capita in the North, and over €3 [euros] [about 4.50 USD] per capita in Scotland, which has seen a 12 per cent reduction in suicide rates in the past three years.

We should bow our heads in shame at our limpid response to youth suicide, the leading cause of death in our young people.

The recently formed Action on Suicide Alliance has called on the government to place this problem as a centre stage priority. It seems shortsighted to lay the problem in the domain of the Department of Health [and Children], as surely the Departments of Education and Science, Social [and Family Affairs], Justice[, Equality and Law Reform], Finance, and of course the Department of the Taoiseach [the Prime Minister] all have a significant responsibility to face this problem, and should be chipping into a dedicated long-term suicide prevention fund for the benefit of the nation.

In summary, we should bow our heads in shame at our limpid response to youth suicide, the leading cause of death in our young people, one of the highest youth suicide rates in Europe, and the single greatest challenge facing the humanity of our 21st century Irish nation.

Periodical Bibliography

The following articles have been selected to supplement the diverse views presented in this chapter.

Robert W. Blum — "Young People: Not as Healthy as They Seem," *Lancet*, September 12, 2009.

Bradley Bouzane — "Cancer, Heart Disease Top Killers," Canwest News Service, December 5, 2008.

Goodarz Danaei et al. — "The Preventable Causes of Death in the United States: Comparative Risk Assessment of Dietary, Lifestyle, and Metabolic Risk Factors," *PLoS Medicine*, April 2009.

Amelia Hill — "Atlas Reveals How You Are Likely to Die: New Maps of Mortality Chart How Geographical Differences Influence the Main Causes of Death," *Observer*, October 19, 2008.

Tom Lasseter — "Biden Had It Right: Rural Russia Is Dying of Poverty, Neglect," McClatchy Newspapers, August 5, 2009.

Daniel Martin — "3,000 Needless Deaths Every Year; Hospital Chairman Sacked After Second Damning Report in a Day," *Daily Mail*, November 28, 2009.

Fred Ouma — "Uganda: The Ten Leading Killers of Country's Men," allAfrica.com, August 24, 2008. http://allafrica.com.

Sabin Russell — "Death Rate Higher When AIDS Treatment Is Erratic; Study a Blow to Idea of Managing HIV by Monitoring White Cells," *San Francisco Chronicle*, November 30, 2006.

Graeme Smith — "Kandahar's Gatekeeper for the Dead," *Globe and Mail*, September 15, 2007.

End-of-Life Care

Worldwide, Organizations View Palliative Care as a Human Right

Frank Brennan

In the following viewpoint, Australian doctor Frank Brennan from Calvary Hospital, Kogarah, New South Wales, argues that palliative care (usually defined as medical care or treatment concentrating on the relief of pain rather than on finding a cure) is a basic human right. He cites documents from the World Health Organization (WHO), the Korea Declaration, and Pope Benedict XVI in support of his contention. He asserts that the international right to health care as articulated by the United Nations and the WHO extends to palliative care.

As you read, consider the following questions:

1. Who is Margaret Somerville, and what was her argument in a 1992 seminal paper, according to Frank Brennan?

2. What are the signers of the International Covenant on Economic, Social, and Cultural Rights (ICESCR) obligated to do concerning health care?

3. What kind of care is best for countries with low resources, according to Brennan, citing general recommendations from the World Health Organization?

Frank Brennan, "Palliative Care as an International Human Right," *Journal of Pain and Symptom Management*, vol. 33, no. 5, May 2007, pp. 494–98. Copyright © 2007 U.S. Cancer Pain Relief Committee. All rights reserved. Reproduced with permission from Elsevier.

Death is inevitable. The provision of good health care at the time of death is less so. Throughout the world, there are wide disparities in the capacity, resources, and infrastructure devoted to the care of people with life-limiting illnesses. The majority of countries have neither formal palliative care[1] policies nor integrated palliative care services, do not meet basic international guidelines in the provision of palliative care, and have legislation or policies whose effect restricts the availability of opioids for medical purposes.

In 1992, Margaret Somerville, a preeminent scholar of medical law, wrote a seminal paper arguing that the relief of suffering is a common goal of both medicine and human rights, and that the relief of the pain and suffering of terminally ill patients is a human right. In recent years, that term has entered the discourse: A Standing Committee of the Canadian Senate, the Cape Town Declaration, the European Committee of Ministers, the International Working Group (European School of Oncology [ESO]), Pope Benedict XVI, and the Korea Declaration have all asserted that palliative care is a fundamental human right.

What, if any, are the foundations for articulating such a right? This article will address one answer to that question: palliative care as an international human right.

The statement that "Palliative Care is a human right" is a powerful one. Does this assertion have any foundation beyond rhetoric? Famously, [18th-century British philosopher] Jeremy Bentham described the articulation of rights without legal foundation as "nonsense on stilts." Is the assertion that there is a right to palliative care "nonsense on stilts?" What, if any, are the foundations of legal rights to palliative care?

Depending on the jurisdiction in which they live, patients with life-limiting illnesses may have a constellation of legal

---

1. Palliative care is usually defined as medical care or treatment concentrating on the relief of pain and symptoms rather than striving to effect a cure for a serious or life-limiting disease.

rights underlying both pain management and palliative care. Health rights derived from national constitutions, the law of negligence, judicial statements on the basis of public interest, and domestic legislation have emerged over the last two decades. They are not within the scope of this article, which is principally concerned with palliative care in the context of international human rights. Any broader discussion of the legal rights founding the provision of palliative care would need to include a discussion of these developments.

The International Human Right to Health Care

The International Covenant on Economic, Social, and Cultural Rights (ICESCR) states:

> Article 12.1. The State Parties to the present Covenant recognise the right of everyone to the enjoyment of the highest attainable standard of physical and mental health.
>
> 2. The steps to be taken . . . to achieve the full realisation of this right shall include those necessary for:
>
> . . . d) The creation of conditions which would assure to all medical service and medical attention in the event of sickness.

In addition, the right to health is articulated in several other international covenants.

The provision of palliative care, where appropriate, is one part of a continuum of health care for all persons.

It is important to emphasize several aspects of this right to health. First, the right is not absolute, to be fulfilled immediately. At its inception, there was a clear recognition that resources varied significantly throughout the world. Rights articulated in this Covenant were seen as aspirational—rights to be achieved progressively over time to the maximum capacity of each signatory nation state. Second, the Covenant imposes obligations solely on governments that are signatories. It does not obligate private citizens, including health professionals. Finally, there is no appeal process or mechanism for complaint. Nevertheless, signatory nations are expected to regularly report to a committee overseeing the Covenant.

There is no express right to palliative care in these United Nations documents. Nevertheless, the World Health Organization [WHO] defines both health and palliative care broadly. Health includes the health of people with life-limiting illnesses. The provision of palliative care, where appropriate, is one part of a continuum of health care for all persons. Therefore, an argument can be made that a right to palliative care can be implied from the overall international human right to health. Assuming that a right to palliative care can be implied from the overall international human right to health, what, correlatively, is the content of the obligation?

The Obligation of Nations to Provide Palliative Care

In 2000, the Committee overseeing the ICESCR issued a General Comment on the right to health, stating what it saw as the "core obligations" of all signatory nations, irrespective of resources. They include obligations to ensure access to health facilities, goods and services on a nondiscriminatory basis; to provide essential drugs as defined by the WHO; and to adopt and implement a national public health strategy. Interpreting this Comment in the context of palliative care, this would oblige nations to ensure a universal access to services, the provision of basic medications for symptom control and terminal care, and the adoption and implementation of national palliative care policies.

For palliative care, a further guide to minimum standards expected by the international community emerges from WHO recommendations. These include that all countries should adopt a national palliative care policy, ensure the training and education of health professionals and promote public awareness, ensure the availability of morphine in all health care settings, and ensure that minimum standards for pain relief and palliative care are progressively adopted at all levels of care. The symmetry is clear: The obligations of governments, as interpreted by the Committee that oversees the international right to health, accords exactly with the recommendations of the preeminent world health body.

Recognizing the widely divergent capacities of countries, the WHO set out general recommendations for different resource settings. For countries with low resource settings, home-based care is probably the best way of achieving good quality care. In countries with medium level resources, services should be provided by primary health care clinics and home-based care. In high resource settings, there is a variety of options, including home-based care.

Many Support Palliative Care

Several international statements have been made, over recent years, asserting that the provision of palliative care is a universal right. Collectively, they represent statements of advocacy and objective. In addition, they provide a sense of the architecture and content of this purported right.

Conscious of the appalling unfolding tragedy of HIV [human immunodeficiency virus]/AIDS [acquired immunodeficiency syndrome], the poorly met needs of cancer patients and the inadequacy of governmental response throughout the African continent, the Cape Town Declaration (2002) asserted four main propositions:

1. Palliative care is a right of every adult and child with a life-limiting disease.

2. Appropriate drugs, including strong opioids, should be made accessible to every patient requiring them in every sub-Saharan country and at all levels of care.

3. The establishment of education programs is necessary at all levels of the learning continuum.

4. Palliative care should be provided at all levels of care. . . . While primary care is emphasized, secondary and tertiary level teams are needed to lead and foster primary level care.

In 2004, the International Working Group (European School of Oncology) released a position paper, "A New International Framework for Palliative Care." It stated that "there should be free access to palliative care . . . for all cancer patients, as a fundamental human right." Based on their definition of palliative care, the ESO Working Group proposed two further refinements that reflect the levels at which palliative care can be delivered: *Basic palliative care*, which should be provided by all health professionals, and *Specialized palliative care* to be provided by a trained multiprofessional team to manage persisting and more complex problems and to provide specialized educational and practical resources to other health professionals.

The Korea Declaration emerged from the 2nd Global Summit of National Hospice and Palliative Care Associations in 2005. It stated that governments must "make access to hospice and palliative care a human right." Specifically, it called on governments to include palliative care as part of health policy; integrate palliative care training into the curricula of health professionals; ensure the availability and affordability of all necessary drugs, especially opioids; and strive to make hospice and palliative care available to all citizens in the setting of their choice.

Another significant international statement that has clear implications for the provision of palliative care was the Montréal Statement on the Human Right to Essential Medicines

(2005). The Statement expressly linked the international right to health with the universal access to these essential medications.

Palliative Care as a Human Right

In his message for the 2006 World Day of the Sick, Pope Benedict XVI stated that an essential emphasis of palliative care was the preservation of human dignity. His Holiness expressly stated that the provision of palliative care services was a human right: ". . . it is necessary to stress once again the need for more palliative care centers, which provide integral care, offering the sick the human assistance and spiritual accompaniment they need. This is a right belonging to every human being, one which we must all be committed to defend."

Synthesizing these sources (the Committee that oversees the international right to health, the WHO and the international palliative care community), a consensus on the content of the obligation on individual governments in relation to palliative care appears to be emerging.

In recent years, a considerable body of literature has concentrated on the right to health, especially in the context of the significant inequalities in access to health care throughout the world. Indeed, to [J.M.] Mann, a pioneering theorist in this area, the promotion and protection of human rights and health are "inextricably linked." Other theorists have been critical of the concept of an individual "right to health," describing it as illusory, meaningless, or, in the context of a world with limited resources, unattainable. Others have emphasized the provision of health care in terms of equality and social justice, or as a foundation of the capability of leading a healthy life.

Despite these debates, critical links have been made between health and human rights by academia, governments,

The Great Need for Palliative Care

When we consider the evidence for the effectiveness of palliative care, the lack of palliative care provision for those who may benefit from it is abysmal. A number of systematic evidence reviews have appraised outcome data from around the world, concluding that palliative care in all its forms (hospice, hospital, home-based care, day care) improves outcomes for patients and families. In addition to that body of evidence, there is a deep humanitarian foundation to palliative care.

Worldwide more than 57 million people died during 2002, of these 7 million died of malignant neoplasm and 2.7 million died of AIDS-related illness. In 2006, UNAIDS [Joint United Nations Programme on HIV/AIDS] estimates that over 40 million people, 2.3 million of whom are under the age of 15 years, are infected with HIV and are living with the disease requiring disease-specific care integrated with palliative care to ensure that physical symptoms, as well as challenging psychosocial and spiritual issues are addressed. Also, there are growing numbers of individuals with other chronic and life-threatening conditions. Throughout the world, millions suffer and die with end-stage cardiac failure, respiratory, renal and hepatic failure. These people are likely to experience problems that would benefit from palliative care at some time.

In developed nations, the prevalence of these conditions will increase with the ageing of the population. In addition, life-limiting neurological conditions such as dementia, amyotrophic lateral sclerosis and cerebrovascular disease contribute to the burden of end-of-life care.

Frank Brennan, Liz Gwyther, and Richard Harding,
Palliative Care as a Human Right, *Open Society Institute Public Health Program, January 2008.*

nongovernmental organizations, and international bodies including agencies of the United Nations. . . .

Palliative Care Is Good Health Care

The World Health Organization and multiple international statements on palliative care have recognized the stark reality: at a global level, specialist palliative care services are rarely available and that in the majority of countries, only the most basic, home-based care is being provided. Clearly, this has implications for any discussion of palliative care as a universal right. Indeed, when one examines the provision of palliative care services internationally, are we not talking about the provision of simply *good health care* that includes palliative care? For if we are focusing on the comfort of a patient with a life-limiting illness, surely that must include water, food, a habitable environment, warmth, bedding, and sanitation as much as symptom control. Indeed, it would be artificial to separate a "right to palliative care" from a general right to health, housing, water, and sanitation. All are interconnected. All determine good health, even and including at the end of life. That interconnectedness was made expressly by the General Comment on the Right to Health.

In promoting a human right to palliative care, there is an immediate problem with interpretation. What exactly does such a right mean? A right to an integrated palliative care service? The right of access to a palliative care inpatient unit? A right to demand any intervention or resource the patient or their family sees fit? The right to a "good" and "dignified" death?

While we are increasingly equipped to deal with the challenges presented to us as health professionals, many aspects of serious illness and death are beyond our control. The right to palliative care can only mean a reasonable and proportionate response to the needs of patients. It can never mean an absolute guarantee that suffering will never occur. If an international obligation was expected at that level, no government could meet it. Equally, at an individual perspective, if the right was placed at a level of perfection, no health professional could possibly fulfill their responsibility to fulfill that right.

It would be artificial to separate a "right to palliative care" from a general right to health, housing, water, and sanitation.

Enforcing the Right to Palliative Care

Other significant limitations to the international human right to health are the issues of adherence and enforcement. The Committee overseeing the Covenant has no powers of enforcement or sanction. Nevertheless, it does have a moral and persuasive capacity. It could reinforce statements already made by other international bodies, including the WHO and the International Narcotics Control Board, recommending that countries liberalize opioid laws [laws that control pain relief drugs such as morphine] and report the true opioid requirements of their population. Furthermore, the Committee could remind signatory nations of their core obligations with respect to health in the context of palliative care.

Another significant agent for persuasion, education, and advocacy is the office of the Special Rapporteur of the Human Rights Commission on the right to health. According to its founding resolution, the Special Rapporteur can receive complaints alleging violations of this right and correspond with the relevant governments to clarify and invite comment and, where appropriate, remind governments of their obligations under international law.

Given the enormous unmet needs of patients with life-limiting illnesses in the world, it is not surprising that advocates have promoted the provision of palliative care as a human right. Indeed, those statements have emerged in an era where links are being generally made between health and human rights. A human right to palliative care may be implied from the international right to health care. However, that right should not be seen in isolation. If the goal is freedom from unnecessary suffering, then the provision of all possible measures to ensure that relief is met must be present—including adequate housing, nutrition, water, and sanitation. For the progressive fulfillment of a human right to palliative care, much will be required: flexible and creative public policy, greater access to opioids for medical purposes, fireless advocacy, comprehensive education, professional leadership, and continued calls upon individual compassion for this most vulnerable group of people.

In Africa, the Aged and Dying Need More Palliative Care

Richard A. Powell, Eve Namissango, Jacquie Teera-Ssentoogo, Boniface N. Mogoi, Julia Downing, Paul Cann, and Faith Mwangi-Powell

In the following viewpoint, Richard A. Powell and others summarize research concluding that aging populations, particularly in Africa, need more access to palliative care to help manage pain. The authors argue that attention to HIV/AIDS in Africa has led to a "crowding out" of attention for the care of the elderly. To address this, they recommend new government policies, more education and training, and increased drug availability. Powell is the monitoring and research manager for the African Palliative Care Association (APCA).

As you read, consider the following questions:

1. According to the viewpoint, what are the two critical components of palliative care, based on Dame Cicely Saunders's statement of the relationship between physical and mental suffering?

2. How has palliative care been traditionally viewed in the care continuum, according to the authors?

3. Why are existing organizations unable to deliver palliative care effectively to their clients, in the authors' view?

Richard A. Powell, Eve Namissango, Jacquie Teera-Ssentoogo, Boniface N. Mogoi, Julia Downing, Paul Cann, and Faith Mwangi-Powell, "Background," *Bridging the Gap: Extending Palliative Care Services to Older People in Two East African Countries*, Kampala, Uganda: African Palliative Care Association, 2008. Copyright © African Palliative Care Association 2008. Reproduced by permission.

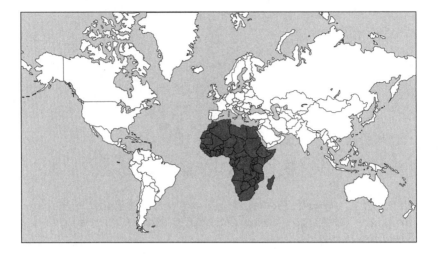

As a consequence of increased life expectancy, it is esti-mated that the number of older people (defined as those people aged 60 years and above), will more than triple globally by 2050, increasing from 606 million in 2000 to a projected 1.9 billion [according to the United Nations]. Moreover, there will also be an increase in the proportion of people constituting the oldest old (i.e. those 80 years or older); whereas they currently comprise 11 per cent of the 60+ age group, this is anticipated to grow to 19 per cent by 2050. Additionally, the number of those people aged 100 years or older is projected to increase 15-fold over a comparable timescale, from approximately 145,000 in 1999 to 2.2 million by 2050.

Whereas 6 out of every 10 older people currently originate in resource-constrained regions of the world, by 2050 this will increase to 80 per cent. In these regions, the proportion of the population aged 60 years or over is estimated to rise from 8 per cent in 2000 to nearly 20 per cent in 2050. The majority of these older persons are women. In resource-constrained countries, there are 85 men for every 100 women over 60; for the over 80s, there are only 73 men for every 100.

Ageing Populations Need Care

Ageing is a process associated with various health-related complications. More specifically, these features of population ageing will increasingly bring important challenges to health care policy makers as the pattern of diseases (i.e. in terms of morbidity and mortality) evident within society change. More specifically, the epidemiological transition will result in an increased importance attached to diseases and fatalities attributable to noncommunicable diseases vis-à-vis infectious diseases.

Recent United Nations (UN) and civil society initiatives—especially the 2002 [UN] Second World Assembly on Ageing and the ensuing Madrid International Plan of Action on Ageing—have stressed that population ageing is a present-day and integral development challenge for Africa that must be addressed, the latter calling for ageing to be included in national social and economic development policies. These global declarations were recently echoed, regionally by the African Union's adoption of the *Africa Health Strategy, 2007–2015* which refers to the alarming rate of growth of chronic diseases linked to noncommunicable demographic changes (including hypertension, stroke, diabetes, and chronic respiratory disease), recognises the role of older people as carers of orphans and vulnerable children (OVC), and calls for the disaggregation of collected data by age and gender to enable more focused action.

Notwithstanding the minimal policy and programmatic advances on such initiatives, in sub-Saharan Africa adaptation of the UN's definition of 'older people' is problematic, often rendered inappropriate to the setting. Indeed, resource-abundant country definitions are often being replaced by more complex, if ultimately, arbitrary, multidimensional sociocultural definitions [according to HelpAid International]:

> In rural situations, where birth registration is poor or even unknown, physical features are commonly used to estimate

a person's age. The colour of a person's hair, failing eyesight and diseases, such as arthritis, are some features used to define an older person. More complex definitions embrace a host of social and cultural issues and may include, for example, the person's seniority status within his/her community and the number of grandchildren which he/she has.

Moreover, the UN definition is commonly associated with legal entitlement to age-specific pension benefits. Considering that the majority of older persons in sub-Saharan Africa live in rural locations and work outside the formal employment sector, with no expectation of receiving formal retirement benefits, this chronological age-based definition has minimal relevance. Moreover, this fact is compounded in those societies where life expectancy is incomparable with those high levels evident in resource-abundant countries.

Problems of the Elderly in Africa

Irrespective of this important definitional distinction and the problems that it gives rise to (e.g. cross-national data noncomparability), there is a growing body of work on the plight of those who are considered aged in the region. In particular, not only do elderly Africans exhibit those debilitating diseases found among the elderly in resource-abundant countries, but the absence of national welfare programmes (e.g. pensions, benefits) and the trend toward urbanization and serious economic stress among the younger adult population, is slowly eroding (if not definitively eliminating) the extended family network. Moreover, older people are normally the primary carers for OVC infected and affected by HIV [human immunodeficiency virus] / AIDS [acquired immunodeficiency syndrome]—in Botswana, Namibia, Malawi, South Africa, Tanzania and Zimbabwe, for example, up to 60 per cent of orphaned children live in grandparent-headed households—for whom they often perform an important health communication role. As the rate of ageing in resource-constrained countries is greater than that in resource-abundant countries, the former will have less time to initiate appropriate societal adaptations to address the multiple consequences of population ageing.

One area of gerontological care provision that has been both neglected and under-researched across the [African] continent is that of palliative care for the aged.

The problems faced by the aged are compounded nationally in many African countries by, for example: limited available expertise in geriatric medicine, which is not taught in many medical and nursing schools; the absence of integrated national policies for the care of the aged; the lack of national councils to coordinate existing and new programmes for the aged; the absence of effective clinical components within many existing care programmes for the aged; and the cross-cutting features of health care systems' functioning (i.e. their limited financial and human resource capacities, their core agendas and priorities, and their specific HIV/AIDS programmatic foci, that has 'crowded out' care for age-related noncommunicable diseases). . . .

Palliative Care and the Aged

In an era where increasing life expectancy rather than improving the quality of life is a stated UN millennium goal for sustainable development, one area of gerontological care provision that has been both neglected and under-researched across the continent is that of palliative care for the aged.

Since its origins in the care of patients in the United Kingdom with advanced malignant disease in the 1960s, palliative care has evolved rapidly in resource-abundant countries from the margins of oncological practice to the centre of mainstream care for those with progressive, life-limiting illnesses.

The World Health Organization (WHO) describes palliative care as:

> An approach that improves the quality of life of patients and their families facing the problems associated with life-threatening illness, through the prevention and relief of suffering by means of early identification and impeccable assessment and treatment of pain and other problems, physical, psychosocial and spiritual.

Based upon [prominent English nurse] Dame Cicely Saunders's articulation of the relationship between physical and mental suffering as 'total pain' (i.e. physical symptoms, mental distress, social problems and emotional difficulties), palliative care essentially has two critical components: pain and symptom control (including the administration of oral morphine for severe opiate-sensitive pain) and supportive care (which attends to the psychological, social, spiritual and cultural needs of both the patient and [his or her] family). As such, it uses non-pharmacologic as well as pharmacologic interventions, attributing equal importance to both to address the holistic needs of the presenting individual. Importantly, non-pharmacologic management is not a substitute for care in settings where drugs are unavailable. Consequently, an organisation only providing one of these two components of palliative care is not providing palliative care in its entirety: pain control without effective psychosocial care is anaesthesiology; psychosocial care without adequate pain control is simply supportive care. Moreover, the needs of people requiring palliative care vary over time, as pressing issues for patients and families surface and disappear, so that the proportion of total care given as disease-modifying / curative treatment (e.g. treatment for opportunistic infections or antiretroviral therapy) and the proportion given as palliative treatment (e.g. pain and symptom control) also varies. Additionally, palliative care has traditionally been viewed as a 'last resort' intervention in the care continuum, to be delivered once a person was considered to be dying, signalled by the ending of the need for curative treatment. However, this traditional view has been replaced by one that sees palliation introduced in the earlier stages of the disease progression in conjunction with disease-modifying treatment as part of an integrated continuum of care. . . .

Palliative Care in Sub-Saharan Africa

To achieve adequate palliative care, the WHO recently recommended an enhanced four-component public health model for delivering palliative care services.

The components of this model are:

Government policy. The national government health and regulatory authorities should establish and support a policy that makes palliative care a high priority in the health care system.

Education / training. The public, policy makers, and regulators should be informed of the benefits of palliative care, and health care professionals should be trained to assess and manage pain using the three-step ladder.

Drug availability. The essential drugs for palliative care, including opioids such as morphine, should be made available.

Implementation. Among opinion leaders, with suitably trained manpower, incorporation into strategic and business plans, and the establishment of palliative care standards, guidelines and measures.

Current provision of palliative care in Africa is, however, patchy, often provided from centres of excellence rather than integrated into the mainstream health care system. Indeed, for the overwhelming majority of Africans who currently endure progressive, life-limiting illnesses, access to culturally appropriate, holistic palliative care (that includes effective pain management) is at best limited, and at worst nonexistent. Sub-Saharan Africa has twice as many deaths per 1,000 head of population annually compared to that of North America,

Doctors Recommend Palliative Care in Africa and the Caribbean

In many resource-poor countries, death is accompanied by avoidable pain and other distressing symptoms. Unfortunately, governments in these countries usually give care at the end of life a low priority compared with preventive and curative services. This prioritization makes little sense, especially when applied to treating patients with cancer and HIV/AIDS, since prevention efforts are often failing to reduce the disease burden, while treatments aimed at cure or prolonging life are still too expensive to be made widely available.

As three physicians in Jamaica, Uganda, and Rwanda, we believe that providing quality care at the end of life should be seen as a global public health priority. . . .

Patients in developing countries often present with far advanced malignant disease, and as many as 80% of people with cancer may be incurable at diagnosis. . . .

About 80% of cancer patients will have pain in the terminal phase of their disease, and we estimate that at least 25% of HIV/AIDS patients have substantial pain during their illness.

Effective and relatively cheap methods exist for controlling pain and other symptoms. For example, the World Health Organization (WHO) has outlined a relatively cheap way of relieving cancer pain in about 90% of patients, which could be extended to patients with HIV/AIDS. Sadly, most people in Africa and the Caribbean who need pain relief aren't receiving it.

Dingle Spence, Anne Merriman, and Agnes Binagwaho,
"Palliative Care in Africa and the Caribbean,"
PLoS Medicine, vol. 1, no. 1, October 19, 2004.

yet only 1.5% of global palliative care resources compared to 55% in the latter. Moreover, a recent survey of hospice and palliative care services on the continent found not only that 44.7% (21/47) of African countries had no identified hospice or palliative care activity, but that only 8.5% (n=4) could be classified as having services approaching some measure of integration with mainstream service providers.

However, the growth of awareness of the need to expand palliative care in sub-Saharan Africa, and the increasing availability of funding to realize that need, have resulted in major developments in patient care in recent years, with increasing numbers of care providers demanding the acquisition of palliative care skills. . . .

Current provision of palliative care in Africa is . . . patchy, often provided from centres of excellence rather than integrated into the mainstream health care system.

Unique Burdens on the Elderly Are Neglected

Whilst there are positive developments occurring in palliative care in Africa, they are primarily associated with addressing the impact of the HIV/AIDS pandemic and with the non-aged. The specific requirements of the African aged (e.g. potentially enduring age-related conditions, compounded by HIV/AIDS, poverty, social isolation, bereavement and loss arising from their children's premature death, and the burden of caring for their grandchildren and/or OVC) are largely neglected. . . .

In a region where finite national budgets face multiple pressing demands, the African aged remain a low priority. Moreover, even where palliative care services exist and provide care for the aged, engaging this 'special population' can prove problematic, especially with respect to HIV/AIDS. [As J. Downing discovered in 2006,]

Older people may not seek care because they fear the stigma of HIV/AIDS as well as because they may be dealing with other health problems. A large number of older people are caring for their children's children, as their own children have died through war, HIV, or famine. Thus a grandmother may be caring for many orphaned grandchildren without support from her own children. For her, finding time and money to obtain her own palliative care is a challenge on top of meeting her grandchildren's essential survival needs. The elderly who have seen their children dying from HIV/AIDS may also fear the disease and believe that 'nothing more can be done for them'. This, along with a belief in 'traditional medicine', means that they may put off accessing palliative care.

Existing organisations for the aged generally lack the specialised skills and experience necessary to deliver palliative care effectively to their clients. Moreover, many of these organisations are financially insecure, small-scale and populated by volunteers.

In Latin America, HIV/AIDS Patients Have Minimal Access to Palliative Care

Open Society Institute

According to the following viewpoint by the Open Society Institute, adults and children suffering from HIV/AIDS experience extreme pain. In Latin America, however, only 5–10 percent of the people who need palliative care receive it. Palliative care in this case includes antiretroviral drugs and pain medication. The author cites several barriers to palliative care in Latin America: Nations lack national health policies, health care professionals are not adequately trained in palliative care, and pain medications are under-prescribed and under-supplied. The Open Society Institute is a private operating and grant-making foundation that works for democratic governance, human rights, and economic, legal, and social reform.

As you read, consider the following questions:

1. What is HAART therapy, as Open Society reports, and is it included in palliative care for HIV/AIDS patients?
2. Which Latin American countries had national palliative care associations at the time this viewpoint was written?

Open Society Institute, *Public Health Fact Sheet: The State of Palliative Care and HIV/ AIDS in Latin America*, Open Society Institute Public Program, International Palliative Care Initiative, July 2008, pp. 1–3. Copyright © 2008 Open Society Institute. Some rights reserved. Reproduced by permission.

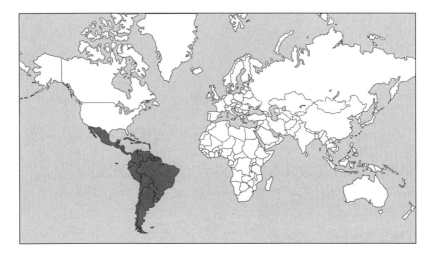

3. Why are doctors, nurses, psychologists, social workers and other health care professionals ill-equipped to provide palliative care, according to the author?

Palliative care, as defined by the World Health Organization [WHO], is "an approach that improves the quality of life of patients and their families facing the problems associated with life-threatening illness, through the prevention and relief of suffering by means of early identification and impeccable assessment and treatment of pain and other problems, physical, psychosocial and spiritual." Palliative care is a vital and necessary component in the care of children and adults living with HIV [human immunodeficiency virus]/AIDS [acquired immunodeficiency syndrome]. It should be delivered concurrently with curative treatment beginning at the time of diagnosis as it helps to alleviate pain and other physical symptoms, as well as address the psychological and social effects that result from living with a life-limiting illness.

HIV/AIDS in Latin America and the Role of Palliative Care

There are currently 1.6 million people reported to be living with HIV/AIDS in Latin America. In 2007, an estimated

100,000 people became infected with HIV and 58,000 died of AIDS. Young adults, ages 15–24, comprise the majority of HIV infections within Latin America, while globally 2.1 million children under the age of 15 are living with HIV. Research has shown that 60–80 percent of patients with HIV/AIDS experience moderate to severe pain during the course of the illness with pain most prevalent in the advanced stages of the illness. Children and adults with HIV/AIDS often suffer from opportunistic infections and a range of symptoms such as fatigue, anorexia, dyspnea, fever, numbness, anxiety, and depression. These symptoms create pain and discomfort, placing an additional burden of physical and psychological distress on the patient and [his or her] family members.

Palliative care must be an essential part of HIV/AIDS care. It serves as a model of care that is patient-centered and focused on relieving pain and other distressing symptoms that are a result of the disease and its treatment. Bereavement care for family members is also an essential component of palliative care.

Of the total number of people who need palliative care services in Latin America, experts estimate that only 5–10 percent receive it, with the majority of services available in large cities, leaving the rural population largely underserviced. UNAIDS [Joint United Nations Programme on HIV/AIDS] reports that globally, palliative care "is one of the most neglected aspects of health care."

Palliative care must be an essential part of HIV/AIDS care.

HAART (highly active antiretroviral therapy) is an integral component of palliative care for children and adults living with HIV/AIDS. Although it does not provide a cure, it can greatly improve a patient's health and quality of life. If delivered early in the course of the illness, HAART can have a positive impact on the trajectory of the disease. HAART can be highly effective in extending the life of a person living with AIDS, with the disease resembling more of a progressive or chronic illness in which palliative care expertise and services are needed to manage pain and symptoms over a longer period of time. Because patients often experience multiple symptoms as side effects during HAART, concurrent palliative care is essential in managing these symptoms. Research data shows that when palliative care is used to treat the pain and symptoms associated with HAART, a patient is more likely to adhere to the prescribed drug regimen and less likely to discontinue treatment. In low-resource countries where patients often present very late in the course of the illness, HAART may not be possible. Palliative care offers the most humane and appropriate response to care for dying patients and their families. It is estimated that 75 percent of the adult population in Latin America has access to HAART, but the level of access for children is less than 35 percent.

The State of Palliative Care in Latin America

Palliative care is provided at a national, regional, and local level and in a variety of settings: hospitals, clinics, hospices, assisted living facilities, and at home. Comprehensive palliative care should be integrated across a continuum of health care services and is delivered by doctors, nurses, community-based home care workers, social workers, psychologists, spiritual leaders, and trained volunteers. Palliative care focuses on the needs of the patient and the family and is coordinated by a team of health care professionals involved in the various aspects of care. Community-based home care models of palliative care for children and adults with HIV/AIDS provide excellent examples of the role of a palliative care team working through trained community health workers in resource-poor settings. These models enable care to take place at the home and support the patient and the family during advanced illness, providing bereavement services to the family following death.

In Latin America, palliative care is at varying levels of development. Currently, Costa Rica, Cuba, and Chile are the only countries that have national health programs that include palliative care. A study conducted by the Latin American Association for Palliative Care [ALCP] found that while 86 percent of respondents reported to have a national HIV/AIDS program in their country, palliative care was included in less than a quarter of them. Of the 35 countries in Latin America and the Caribbean there are only eight countries—Argentina, Brazil, Colombia, Costa Rica, El Salvador, Paraguay, Peru, and Uruguay—that have a national palliative care association. Access to essential palliative care drugs is also very limited; for example, morphine, an inexpensive and highly effective opioid used as the mainstay of therapy to treat pain in patients with cancer or AIDS, is widely underused in Latin America with an average consumption rate of 0.8723 mg in 2006, well below the global mean of 5.98 mg, and less than one percent of the global consumption.

Access to essential palliative care drugs is . . . very limited; for example, morphine . . . is widely underused in Latin America.

Barriers to Palliative Care

Lack of a national health policy, lack of drug policies to assure the availability of essential medicines, and lack of education of health care professionals and the public are the three main barriers to the provision and delivery of palliative care. Health care professionals are often lacking the necessary training to assess pain and administer opioids properly for patients with HIV/AIDS, or fail to prescribe these drugs because they are fearful of addiction or misuse. As a result, opioids are under-

Relief of Pain for Dying South Americans

In palliative care, one of the basic principles is the relief of pain with the use of the WHO analgesic ladder [pain management guidelines established by WHO] and the use of opioids. All the South American countries have adopted the WHO guidelines. However, changes in legislation and regulations are urgently needed to allow adequate access to opioids.

There are still some difficulties with the treatment of cancer pain in this region. The health policy does not endorse opioid analgesics. As a result, many cancer patients still die with their pain uncontrolled. Additionally, patients and their families retain many taboos related to the use of these opioids, necessitating that the palliative care teams spend much time educating the family about the use of opioids such as morphine.

There are many myths regarding palliative care, and still many health care professionals who do not know how to adequately assess and treat pain. The misplaced fear of respiratory depression or hastening death through the use of opioids remains common. Opioid phobia among regulators is illustrated through their concern that making opioids available for therapeutic use would increase the illicit drug market.

Although opioids can be easily found in the capital cities, prescriptions for controlled substances require many copies. Ready availability of opioids is not a reality for the inner-country people. These people must come to the capital city to get opioid medications for pain relief.

Marta H. Junin, "Palliative Care in South America,"
Textbook of Palliative Nursing, 2nd ed., eds. Betty R. Ferrel
and Nessa Coyle, New York: Oxford University Press, 2006, p. 1196.

prescribed and under-supplied in pharmacies and hospitals, making them unavailable or inaccessible to the patients who need them.

Palliative care must be integrated into national health care systems to work successfully and not be delivered as a separate service of care. National health care plans and policies often do not include palliative care or the necessary and balanced regulatory drug policies that allow for the proper delivery of pain and symptom management. As a result, palliative care is not integrated into delivery systems.

Palliative care is often not included in the curriculum at medical universities or nursing colleges, leaving doctors, nurses, psychologists, social workers, and other health care professionals ill-equipped to deliver the type of care needed for patients and their families. Data from surveys show that many countries in Latin America do not recognize palliative care as a medical specialty or discipline.

Countries that want to integrate palliative care as a part of their national health care system need to develop national policies for palliative care, and include palliative care in national AIDS plans. National drug policies must ensure opioid availability and accessibility for patients. Legal frameworks need to be put in place that outline and promote palliative care development and financing, implement and integrate palliative care services across public and private health care systems, and include palliative care in professional education.

Policy makers need to ensure that essential medicines, such as morphine, are not restricted by drug policies that inhibit the affordability, accessibility, and availability for patients and are distributed in both urban and rural areas. Laws should also ensure that prescribing policies are efficient so as not to delay the delivery of medication to patients in pain. Health care professionals should be able to prescribe in doses that are recommended and considered necessary by international health bodies, such as the World Health Organization. Palliative care education must be included in the training of health care professionals and part of all national health care strategies, including national cancer and HIV/AIDS plans.

Palliative Care Is Essential

Health care professionals need to recognize the importance of palliative care as an essential component to HIV/AIDS care or any treatment of a life-limiting illness, and that it begins for the patient at the time of diagnosis. The health care professionals who treat patients with HIV/AIDS need to be trained in palliative care to deliver the best and most comprehensive level of care for their patients. In order for a palliative care curriculum to become an integrated part of training in undergraduate and graduate education, health care professionals must become advocates and leaders who can call attention to this critical gap in service delivery.

Italy Is Slow to Adopt Palliative Care

Francesca Crippa Floriani

Francesca Crippa Floriani, president of the Federazione di Cure Palliative (FCP), or the Palliative Care Federation, of Milan, Italy, summarizes the growth of the Italian palliative care movement in the viewpoint that follows. She asserts that although there are more programs to provide this care, there are not enough trained professionals to staff them. In addition, she argues that many people are not receiving adequate pain medication because of the "opiumphobia" of many Italian doctors. She describes the founding of the FCP in 1999 and praises the work of its volunteers. She concludes by noting the yearly contributions made to palliative care by the FCP.

As you read, consider the following questions:

1. To what does Francesca Crippa Floriani attribute Italian distrust of opioids?

2. How many nonprofit organizations make up the membership of the Palliative Care Federation?

3. As the author reports, how many people in Italy die yearly from incurable disease?

Francesca Crippa Floriani, "European Insight: FCP: Why Italy Is a Special Case When It Comes to Palliative Care," *European Journal of Palliative Care*, vol. 16, no. 4, July 14, 2009. Copyright © 2009 Hayward Group Ltd. Reproduced by permission.

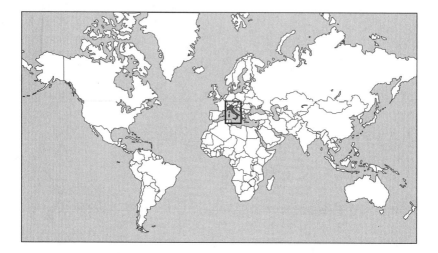

The Start of the Hospice Movement

The development of palliative care in Italy got off to a slow start in comparison with other European countries. However, in recent years, things have begun to change more rapidly, particularly with regard to the establishment of hospices. Ten years ago, we had just one. In 2008, there were more than 150.

The rise in the number of home care services has been slower. In 2005, there were 121 palliative care units; in 2008, the figure had grown to 161. This slowness is probably partly due to the lack of laws, at national and local level, favouring the development of palliative home care.

Since 1999, post-doctorate courses in palliative care (less than a dozen) have been set up in universities to train doctors, nurses, psychologists, social workers and other health and social care professionals, giving them a systematic, in-depth knowledge of palliative care. As yet, however, there are insufficient educational opportunities to train enough staff for the new hospices.

The fact that palliative care is not a recognised medical specialty in Italy creates further problems for doctors seeking a career in this field. In fact, to practise in a hospital, doctors must have a degree in another medical specialty—usually ana-esthesiology, oncology or geriatrics.

Palliative care needs to be formally recognised as a medical specialty. This would enable hospices to gain more experience and improve the competence level of their staff. It is also essential that more hospices are created, so that they spread throughout the northern and central regions of the country and reach southern Italy in suitable numbers.

> *As yet . . . there are insufficient educational opportunities to train enough staff for the new hospices [in Italy].*

What Needs to Be Done

Over the next few years, health care professionals, decision makers and not-for-profit organisations will have to tackle a fundamental task: the creation of a coordinated and efficient care network that can guarantee timely and competent assistance, in the most suitable setting, for chronically or terminally ill patients and their families.

Not only will this network need to provide patients and families with adequate care, but it will also need to give them assistance in managing the difficult aspects of everyday life. At the same time, it will have to ensure a smooth passage between the different care settings, taking care of the bureaucratic aspects so that these are not a burden for patients and their families.

Italy's Opiumphobia

A specific problem that sets Italy apart from most other European countries is the so-called opiumphobia that still prevails. Many doctors—and not just general practitioners—are still fiercely resistant to prescribing opioids for alleviating pain, especially cancer pain. This is matched by a high level of mistrust among patients, who are often reluctant to start an opioid therapy even when it has been prescribed to them.

There are many causes for this distrust of opioids, but the main one is cultural, conditioned by a persistent denial of the seriousness of disease and terminal illnesses. It is often difficult to deal openly with matters related to palliative care because, to date, there is a great resistance to talking about prognoses of terminal illnesses among families and patients, and consequently among doctors and patients. Palliative care is seen as a defeat and, as such, is to be postponed for as long as possible.

Another reason for the distrust of opioids is that palliative care professionals do not receive appropriate training, at university or post-doctoral level, on the efficacy and safety of opioids and, therefore, do not have the necessary knowledge to feel comfortable using them.

Many doctors—and not just general practitioners—are still fiercely resistant to prescribing opioids for alleviating pain, especially cancer pain.

The Role of Not-for-Profit Organisations

Until about ten years ago, there was very little care or support for terminally ill patients provided through the public health or welfare systems. With rare exceptions, the only coordinated, continuous services were organised by not-for-profit organisations at local and community levels. These organisations were mainly run by volunteers. Over time, they have become service suppliers, directly financing and organising the home palliative care teams or partly financing pilot projects of Italy's national welfare system.

In the absence of publicly available information about incurable illnesses issued by the mass media and institutions, not-for-profit organisations began to inform the public on the rights of dying patients by organising studies, seminars and other events throughout the country. For many years, this was the only information at hand.

From the start, not-for-profit organisations have strongly supported those scientific sectors that are striving to promote the principles of palliative medicine (and more generally of pain relief) among palliative care professionals, doctors, nurses and psychologists. By attending training courses, the volunteers indirectly became an authoritative source of information for the movement against unnecessary pain and in favour of the right to be adequately cared for when a cure is not possible.

The Creation of the Palliative Care Federation

It was against this social, cultural and organisational background that the Palliative Care Federation (Federazione di Cure Palliative, FCP) was established, in 1999, by 22 not-for-profit organisations that had been working for many years in the palliative care sector.

Today, the FCP has more than 60 member organisations (out of a total of 140 not-for-profit organisations operating in this field in Italy), characterised by their common mission to provide the best possible support for those in advanced and terminal phases of incurable illnesses, and for their families.

The FCP member organisations offer concrete support, both in terms of information and care. They cooperate with health and social care institutions, with the aim of avoiding needless pain for the more than 250,000 people who die every year in Italy from incurable disease.

As well as helping terminally ill patients and supporting family members who look after patients at the end of life, the FCP disseminates the most relevant information in the field of palliative care and pain relief, among its members and the wider public. It favours the exchange of experience and knowledge at all levels.

Since 2002, the FCP has had an Internet site (www.fedcp.org). The site, which is aimed at both FCP mem-

Italian Doctors Believe Children Should Receive Palliative Care

Children with life-limiting and life-threatening illnesses that lead to death or a life of severe disability deserve a profound cultural and organizational reappraisal of how we care for them when the aim of care is not to make them recover, but to offer the best possible "health" and "quality of life", despite their disease.

Infants, children and adolescents with life-limiting and life-threatening illnesses need support and long-term care in a palliative setting.

The World Health Organization defines palliative care for children as "the active total care of the child's body, mind and spirit, . . . also involves giving support to the family. It begins when illness is diagnosed, and continues regardless of whether or not a child receives treatment directed at the disease". Pediatric palliative care is concerned with the medical, psychosocial, spiritual and economic needs of patients and their families, providing complex patient care solutions involving all aspects of the health care system. . . .

It is important to draw a distinction between palliative care and terminal care: The latter refers to looking after children and their parents during a time closely related to their death (within weeks, days or hours). Terminal care is not palliative care, but palliative care includes terminal care. . . .

For a long time, pediatric patients were not offered palliative care and, even nowadays, only a minimal part of the children with incurable disease can benefit from palliative care in Europe.

Franca Benini et al., "Pediatric Palliative Care," Italian Journal of Pediatrics, vol. 34, no. 4, December 1, 2008, pp. 4–13.

bers and the general public, contains practical information—including the addresses of Italy's home care centres and hospices—as well as constantly updated information on regional, national and international laws, on pain relief, and on associations working in the field. The site also carries information on training courses, especially those aimed at volunteers.

The not-for-profit organisations of the FCP represent the most effective link between the citizens and the institutions working in the field of palliative care. To date, they are the best-placed to convey to the institutions—and to all palliative care professionals involved in providing assistance to terminally ill patients—what is really needed in terms of training, funding and recognition.

The FCP assumes a vigilant role to ensure that the ethics and principles of solidarity that underlie palliative care are not restrained by the logic of economics or profit.

An Annual Day Against Suffering

The FCP has always identified the fight against pain and suffering as one of its main objectives. For this reason, it has dedicated 11 November each year to this commitment. This day is known as 'The day against useless pain in the incurable person'. In recent years, on that day, the actions listed below have been organised.

- In 2001, the day was dedicated to the rights of the terminally ill patient, and a petition to the government was organised in support of a 'Charter of rights for the dying person'.

- In 2002, the FCP wrote the 'Decalogue of the family rights in taking care of the incurable patient', which was signed by 40,000 people.

- In 2003, the chosen topic was 'Suffering in the incurable elderly patient', one of the crucial issues in fighting pain.

- In 2004, a press conference was organised with the then Italian Minister for Health Girolamo Sirchia, who was presented symbolically with all the signatures that had been collected in previous years, which numbered about 80,000. On that occasion, the minister announced that Italian citizens would no longer have to pay for painkillers, including opioids.

- In 2005, a project called 'Living without pain: from hospital to home' was promoted. Fundamental requisites for palliative care, such as continuity of care, were highlighted.

- In 2006, the topic was 'Less bureaucracy for the use of opioids against pain'. The FCP, together with the Italian Society of Palliative Care (Società Italiana di Cure Palliative, SICP), organised a petition to the government to make the prescription of opioids less complex and to eliminate the potentially negative connotations of their therapeutic use.

Italy still does not have a specific law for palliative care.

- In 2007, a new petition to the government was organised to request that, after the great steps taken to build hospices, the same commitment should be shown to develop home palliative care services in the country.

- In 2008, after a thorough review of the work carried out in recent wars, the FCP once again invited the not-for-profit organisations to organise a petition to present to the government. The aim was to inform citizens about, and involve them in, what still needs to be achieved to improve the palliative care network—for example, developing home care and training health care professionals. A specific request was the abolition of the special prescription pads required for opioids for therapeutic use, which are a very complex and bureaucratic way of prescribing opioids to patients. Abolishing them would make it easier for doctors to deliver these drugs.

This year, a new petition will be presented to the government, with the aim of enforcing the 'essential assistance level'. This means that all medical services will be at the expense of the government and free of charge for citizens.

Italy still does not have a specific law for palliative care; the FCP is committed to collaborating with the current government to put one in place.

In the United States, Physician-Assisted Death Is Controversial

Nathanael Johnson

In the following viewpoint, Nathanael Johnson interviews a medical doctor who has been active in the Death with Dignity movement. The doctor recounts how he was approached by people dying from cancer and asked to supply barbiturates. Although he eventually left his practice, he has continued to work with the dying. He believes that people should talk more openly about their choices, but he also believes that people should have control over their own lives and deaths. Johnson is a journalist based in San Francisco.

As you read, consider the following questions:

1. How many people in Oregon have received lethal medication and how many have used it between 1997 and 2007, according to Johnson?

2. What has the Death with Dignity movement morphed into, according to Johnson?

3. What does "Dr. Francis" call Michigan doctor Jack Kevorkian?

Nathanael Johnson, "Perfect Ending: An Extraordinary Passionate Doctor's Career-Long Struggle with the Issue of Death and Dying," *ELDR*, Summer 2008, p. 36. Copyright © 2008 ELDR Media Group, LLC. Reproduced by permission.

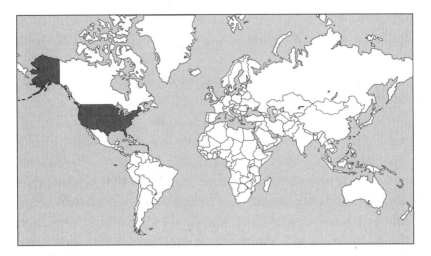

The first time Dr. Francis [name has been changed] killed it was easy. It's often said that for a soldier, the first kill is the hardest. Then it gets easier, until you don't even see a human at the end of your barrel: The optic nerve hands the image of an attacker directly to trigger finger, bypassing the portion of the brain that considers pros and cons. But Francis was a doctor, not a soldier. And for him, it was just the opposite: The first few times it seemed so simple. The patients were comatose and dying anyway. He just turned up the morphine drip and sped them along.

Then the postmaster came along, and mercy killing got complicated.

The post office she ran in that little town was no more than a trailer on the side of the road, lined with fake wood paneling and a few rows of brass boxes. She kept an electric heater by her desk. Every day she would wheel her oxygen tank out to her Oldsmobile, lower herself into the seat and drive to work. It was only a few hundred yards, but she was too short of breath to walk that distance anymore.

A Plea for Help

Dr. Francis knew all this when he stopped in to check the mail that day. They were all neighbors in that town, and it was hard not to know each other's business. He waved hello, took the letters from his box, and asked if she had anything else for him.

"Actually," he remembers her saying in her smoker's voice, "there is something."

She was dying, she explained. It was getting harder and harder to breathe. Her emphysema was only getting worse. And the lung cancer, well, the cancer had won. There would be no more chemotherapy. Her doctors had told her there was nothing else they could do for her. With the doctors gone, that left her alone. As she saw it, there was only one more thing she could do about her labored breathing. That's why she was asking Dr. Francis if he would get her enough barbiturates to put her gently to sleep and stop the wheezing permanently.

Looking back, years later, Dr. Francis shrugs. "I thought her request was reasonable. She was saying, 'Hey I can't take it now, and it's going to get worse. Let me get out of here.' And it—it just seemed intellectually reasonable. And, I think, emotionally reasonable." Then he stops, struck by the strangeness of the moment in retrospect: "Funny that that conversation would happen in a post office."

Post office transactions are constrained to the most trivial of exchanges. A few cents for a stamp. A few words about the weather. The color of the curb outside limits the length of conversations. Yet there they were, making arrangements to determine the question of existence for this woman. A week or so later he gave her the pills.

Although she was circumspect, word got around. Before long, others approached Dr. Francis, and he gave them what they wanted. The way things were going, he could have become an undercover Jack Kevorkian [a Michigan doctor convicted of murder for physician-assisted suicides]—helping people die without the media spectacle. But Dr. Francis bristles when I compare him to the doctor who has assisted in at least

45 deaths. "He's a pervert," Dr. Francis protests. "He's insane. No, I was just interested in helping this woman end her suffering. If I could have found another way to end it without . . ." he pauses, then settles on the bluntest way of putting it, "without killing her, I would have."

Kevorkian is a polarizing figure. Many in the Death with Dignity movement regard him as a hero, while those who believe in the inalienable sanctity of life see him as a monster. Dr. Francis has far more in common with the former group than the latter; he believes in personal liberties and likes to poke fun at religious dogma. But on this issue, Dr. Francis has a weight of experience that keeps him from being polarized.

The doctor's hair and beard are white these days and neatly cropped. He wears rimless glasses which magnify his eyes, giving him a vaguely owlish look. We sit in his living room, holding cups of herbal tea. It has grown dark in the room as the light fades outside. He chuckles. "If I was somewhat [like] Kevorkian, it was in my ignorance."

The Mind-Body Connections

It came as no surprise to him when he heard the postmaster died—but the way she died was surprising. She never took the pills. Intrigued, Dr. Francis inquired after the other people to whom he'd prescribed barbiturates. Not a single one had hastened their death.

And so began a small mystery: What had made every single one of these people choose the long decline they had once so desperately wanted to avoid? What had changed to make the end of their lives more fulfilling? Another doctor might have puzzled over this a while, then shrugged it off. But for Dr. Francis, this mystery took on a special significance. At that point in his life he had begun to question his role as a physician and was looking for lessons. "I was running an ER [emergency room] at the time, so I could see [all kinds of people]—people who drank, people who smoked a lot, people who ate

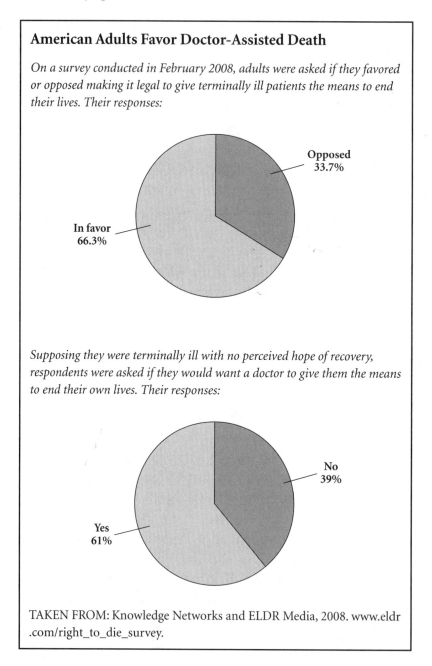

American Adults Favor Doctor-Assisted Death

On a survey conducted in February 2008, adults were asked if they favored or opposed making it legal to give terminally ill patients the means to end their lives. Their responses:

Opposed
33.7%

In favor
66.3%

Supposing they were terminally ill with no perceived hope of recovery, respondents were asked if they would want a doctor to give them the means to end their own lives. Their responses:

No
39%

Yes
61%

TAKEN FROM: Knowledge Networks and ELDR Media, 2008. www.eldr .com/right_to_die_survey.

too much, people who were accident prone, people who had trouble with relationships. I started seeing that their sicknesses or injuries didn't come out of a vacuum. And yet we had no handle on how they lived. We put Band-Aids on them and sent them back to the same crap. I began to see that I was mainly trained as a mechanic. Really what I was operating was a high-tech turnstile."

Perhaps it's obvious, Dr. Francis says, but at the time it was fascinating to discover that a person's culture, their values and priorities in life, the way they conducted their relationships, their fears and aspirations—that all these airy intangibles—could result in real, visible, bodily harm. And, he reasoned, this relationship should work in reverse as well: A patient's mind should be able to salve the afflictions of the flesh. After all, those people to whom he had prescribed pills had somehow found a way to cope with their own suffering after the tools of physical medicine had been exhausted.

[For those suffering from terminal illness], the real cause of their suffering . . . was loss of control.

The Need for Control

This line of reasoning dovetailed with Dr. Francis's theory about what had happened with those people who'd asked him for suicide drugs: He'd made the wrong diagnosis. Dr. Francis had diagnosed life as the cause of their suffering and provided the appropriate prescription. But the real cause of their suffering, Dr. Francis thinks, was loss of control. Fortunately, his prescription provided a kind of off-label effect: "Those pills—having that parachute in hand—gave them a sense of control. And that sense of control—maybe it was just the illusion of control—but it was enough to evaporate that particular kind of suffering. The result is that people wanted to be around longer."

Hospice workers, doctors, and Death with Dignity advocates have told me that people die like they have lived. The people who make plans to hasten their death have often lived a life of exacting discipline. Terminal sickness often robs patients of control—control of their daily schedules, control of their bodies, control of their minds. Having this one last piece of power—power over of time of death—may ease the frustration that comes with loss of control. Numbers from Oregon, which legalized physician-assisted dying in 1997, support this idea. [Washington became the second U.S. state to legalize physician-assisted suicide in November 2008.] In the decade after the law passed, 459 people have received lethal medication and 292 used it.

Eventually Dr. Francis's doubts led him away from medical practice, but his interest kept him around the fringes. One day a group of cancer patients asked him to give some advice about pain control, and he stuck around afterward to watch. It was about what you'd expect: People would talk about what the doctors had told them, chat about the way they felt, make dark jokes about their common situation, and solicit advice. But there was something in this that interested Dr. Francis. So much so that he asked permission to come to the next meeting. He kept attending for the next five years.

Many people agree that suffering doesn't need to be [a] part of dying.

In these meetings Dr. Francis watched as the cancer patients slowly unraveled the snarled threads of their fear, sadness, and self-pity. Often these strands led to the least expected places. The true source of suffering might have less to do with the indignities of dying than with fear of leaving a life unfinished, some loose end untied. But the most interesting thing Dr. Francis saw was that once people understood what was eating at them, they could act on it. There was almost always a way to end suffering.

The Growth of End-of-Life Care

Dr. Francis wasn't the only one to see this. While he was doing his soul searching, end-of-life care was evolving along parallel lines with the hospice movement. Back when Dr. Francis was young, end-of-life care was almost nonexistent. The postmaster's doctors had said, "There's nothing more we can do for you." Today doctors tell their patients that, while they may not be able to make them live forever, hospice can almost guarantee a pain-free death.

Interestingly, the Death with Dignity movement followed a similar path. When Dr. Francis was handing out pills, the Hemlock Society was the leading organization in the Death with Dignity movement. The pages of its newsletters were filled with plans for suicide machines and detailed recipes for ending life. Since then it has morphed into Compassion & Choices, which places the focus on providing options and ending suffering, rather than simply providing the means for death.

Today, many people agree that suffering doesn't need to be [a] part of dying. But there's still plenty of room for disagreement. Dr. Francis thinks that those who advocate physician-assisted death may be too quick to dismiss the process of dying as an important part of life. And on the other side, he thinks the medical establishment still tends to focus on technical fixes with such blinkered obstinacy that it sometimes misses what the patient really wants. "As soon as you put on the white coat you start thinking a little differently," he says. Dr. Francis remembers a meeting in which oncologists were consulting about a patient's breast cancer. The patient had said she didn't want surgery for any reason, yet as the doctors took in her information and began to reason out the possible treatments, that bit of data failed to penetrate.

Seeing the Whole Person

"And they all said, 'The only thing we can see here is surgery,'" says Dr. Francis. "They were thinking about how to fix the problem, not about what is good for the patient. And these are truly wonderful people. They care about their patients. They are personally warm. But you have to devote monastic time to keeping up with information in the field. The nature of our medical system is such that doctors must immediately come up with a solution, then move on. And that allows for our amazing technical expertise. But if you only see the problem, that obscures the real person."

I ask Dr. Francis if this is what bothers him about Kevorkian—that he was so willing to provide a solution to the problem without taking the time to see the real person in front of him.

"Well, he doesn't know anything about the people. He just shows up in his van: 'All right, who wants this?' It's like he's running a drive-through, for Christ's sake," Dr. Francis says.

Assisted dying, I suggest, fits perfectly into a medical system based on physical solutions. It's the last available technical fix. If you follow Western medicine to its logical conclusion, it only makes sense to find Kevorkian there.

Dr. Francis nods, "You could call him the living end."

Assisted dying . . . fits perfectly into a medical system based on physical solutions. It's the last available technical fix.

Talking About Dying

Dr. Francis's work with cancer patients provides a glimpse into how a medical system that is not focused on physical solutions might work. He begins by asking his patient: What bothers you about having cancer?

"Of course I don't say it that way," he explains. "You can't ask straight on or people get pissed. You're supposed to understand that having cancer really bothers people. OK, cool, but what about it bothers you? After they talk about it a while they usually say, 'What bothers me about it is I'm worried I'm gonna die.' All right, next question: What bothers you about dying?"

Figuring this out can take weeks. "It's not the kind of conversation you can have in a post office," Dr. Francis says. And the answers people give are often revelatory. "Eventually you might come back and say, 'I've thought about it for a while and what bothers me is I have unfinished business with my son," Dr. Francis says. "Well, vaya con Dios [Spanish for "go with God"], dude! Go do it."

Ways of Relieving Pain

Of course, things don't always come to such a tidy conclusion. Sometimes people would literally rather die than walk down the dark corridors of their souls to find some source of pain. Dr. Francis thinks that there's almost always a way to relieve suffering—but that's almost. There are always exceptions. He's humble enough to know that his philosophy won't work for everyone.

Dr. Francis has changed in the 40-plus years since he gave a prescription of barbiturates to the postmaster of that small town. He says he probably wouldn't do that today. While his thoughts on this dilemma are now much more nuanced than they were when he was young, one thing hasn't changed: He still thinks that the doctor he was all those years ago should have the right to prescribe those pills if that's what the patient requests.

"As far as what goes on in that little room, I don't think the law should be there. That's the closest thing we have to confessionals in secular society. The problem is doctors don't have priestly training," Dr. Francis says.

And the problem here, as he sees it, lies not with the doctors but with the society that cedes only that one small space for conversations about death.

"If we were truly a civilized society, we'd talk to each other long before we considered suicide. We'd have community networks. Part of the reason we talk about law and torts so much in the U.S. is we've lost so much of our community. In the old days if you were even out of sorts everyone knew about it and they'd drop off a lasagna for you. And now people are much more anonymous and less educated in speaking their feelings."

Medical technology continues to offer more options for extending life, which means that more people are going to have choices about how they die. To make this new technology a blessing rather than a burden, people will have to re-learn a very old technology: the art of having a conversation about death that lasts longer than a 20-minute parking limit.

In the United Kingdom, Terminally Ill Patients Leave the Country in Search of Life-Ending Drugs

AP Online

In the following viewpoint, AP Online *discusses the case of Sir Edward Downes and his wife, who traveled to Zurich to end their lives in the Dignitas clinic, because assisted suicide and euthanasia are illegal in Britain. Cases like these spur attempts to change the law, but such attempts have been repeatedly defeated, despite a lax enforcement of existing law. The Associated Press is a not-for-profit news cooperative, owned by its American newspaper and broadcast members, with the mission to be the essential global news network, providing distinctive news services of the highest quality, reliability, and objectivity.*

As you read, consider the following questions:

1. What reasons did Sir Edward Downes have for choosing to end his life, according to the article?
2. According to *AP Online,* what do critics of Dignitas accuse the group of promoting?
3. How much does Dignitas charge for assisting a suicide, as *AP Online* reports?

"Conductor Downes, Wife Die in Swiss Suicide Clinic," *AP Online*, July 14, 2009. Copyright © 2009 Associated Press. All rights reserved. This material may not be published, broadcasted, rewritten, or redistributed. Reproduced by permission.

British maestro Edward Downes, who conducted the BBC Philharmonic and the Royal Opera but struggled in recent years as his hearing and sight failed, has died with his wife at an assisted suicide clinic in Switzerland. He was 85 and she was 74.

The couple's children said Tuesday that they died "peacefully and under circumstances of their own choosing" on Friday at a Zurich clinic run by the group Dignitas. . . .

"After 54 happy years together, they decided to end their own lives rather than continue to struggle with serious health problems," said a statement from the couple's son and daughter, Caractacus and Boudicca.

"Lady Downes was terminally ill, Sir Edward wasn't. . . . It was a decision they both reached."

The statement said Downes, who became Sir Edward when he was knighted by Queen Elizabeth II in 1991, had "a long, vigorous and distinguished career," but in recent years had become almost blind and nearly deaf.

His wife Joan, a former dancer, choreographer and television producer, had devoted years to working as his assistant.

Downes's manager, Jonathan Groves, said Joan Downes had been diagnosed with terminal cancer.

"Lady Downes was terminally ill, Sir Edward wasn't," he said. "It was a decision they both reached. Sir Edward would have survived her death but he decided he didn't want to. He didn't want to go on living without her."

Groves said he was shocked by the couple's deaths but called their decision "typically brave and courageous."

He said Edward Downes was "a man of extraordinary self-determination in his absolutely uncompromising pursuit of achieving the highest standards musically," who had struggled in old age as his eyesight and hearing failed.

London's Metropolitan Police force said it had been notified of the deaths, and was investigating.

Roughly 100 foreigners—most of them terminally ill—come to Switzerland each year to take advantage of the country's liberal laws on assisted suicide.

The double suicide is the latest in a series of high-profile cases that have spurred calls for a legal change in Britain, where assisted suicide and euthanasia are banned.

More than 100 Britons have died in Swiss clinics run by Dignitas. The organization was established in 1998, and takes advantage of the country's liberal laws on assisted suicide, which suggest that a person can be prosecuted only if they are acting out of self-interest.

Roughly 100 foreigners—most of them terminally ill—come to Switzerland each year to take advantage of the country's liberal laws on assisted suicide. Some are healthy except for a disability or severe mental disorder. Typically they go to a room run by Dignitas, which provides them with a lethal drink of barbiturates. In five minutes they fall asleep—and never wake up.

Other countries, including the Netherlands and Belgium, and the states of Oregon and Washington in the United States, allow the incurably sick to obtain help from a doctor to hasten their death.

But only Switzerland, in a law dating back to 1942, permits foreigners to come and kill themselves. Other organizations provide such services for Swiss residents, but Dignitas is the main organization for foreigners.

Critics accuse Dignitas of promoting "suicide tourism."

Dignitas says it is meeting the needs of its members. It says it charges 10,000 Swiss francs ($9,200) for its services, which include taking care of legal formalities and arranging consultations with a doctor willing to prescribe the barbiturates.

British law is clearly against assisted suicide, but enforcement has been somewhat lax.

British courts have been reluctant in recent years to convict people who help loved ones travel to clinics abroad to end their lives. No relative or friend of any of the Britons who have died in Dignitas clinics has been prosecuted.

But parliamentary efforts to change the rules have all been defeated—most recently last week, when Parliament's upper chamber, the House of Lords, voted down an amendment that would have relaxed the prohibition on assisted dying.

Parliamentary efforts to change the rules have all been defeated—most recently . . . Parliament's upper chamber, the House of Lords, voted down an amendment that would have relaxed the prohibition on assisted dying.

Sarah Wootton, chief executive of campaign group Dignity in Dying, said the Downeses' deaths showed the need to regulate assisted suicide.

Edward Downes is one of the most prominent Britons to have traveled to Switzerland because of its open attitude toward foreigners seeking to end their lives.

He was born in 1924 in Birmingham in central England. He studied at Birmingham University, the Royal College of Music and under German conductor Hermann Scherchen.

In 1952 he joined London's Royal Opera House as a junior staffer—his first job was prompting soprano Maria Callas. He made his debut as a conductor with the company the following year and went on to become associate music director. Throughout his life he retained close ties to the Royal Opera, conducting almost 1,000 performances of 49 different operas there over more than 50 years.

He also had a decades-long association with the BBC Philharmonic Orchestra, where he became principal conductor and later conductor emeritus.

Groves said that during Downes's 70s and 80s, he slowly went blind, "which was a huge problem professionally—not being able to read scores. That had become much worse in recent years.

"His hearing was also deteriorating, which was another problem."

The couple is survived by their children and family said there would be no funeral.

In the United Kingdom, End-of-Life Care Provides for a Home Death

Melanie Henwood

In the following viewpoint, Melanie Henwood discusses a British end-of-life project that provides care for people so that they can stay in their homes or apartments. Specifically, she describes "extra-care housing schemes," and what it requires to allow dying tenants to remain at home. She contrasts the support available to the dying in extra-care housing with those who are in residential care homes and nursing homes. She concludes that helping people remain in their extra-care housing situation is a good option. Henwood is the founder of the Melanie Henwood Associates Health & Social Care Consultancy.

As you read, consider the following questions:

1. According to the viewpoint, what percentage of deaths in the United Kingdom occurs in hospitals?
2. What percentage of extra-care tenants does Henwood assert had their wishes met to die at home?
3. What recommendations does the pilot project described by Henwood make to ensure a good death for extra-care tenants?

Melanie Henwood, "Dying with Dignity," *Community Care*, November 6, 2008, pp. 34–35. Copyright © 2008 Reed Business Information. Reproduced by permission.

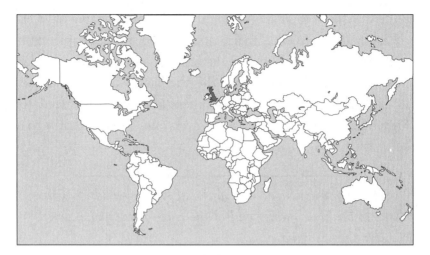

Highlight: In a society where experiences of dying are often a taboo subject, an end-of-life project focuses on allowing people to die at home with good care. Melanie Henwood describes the results.

Abstract. In early 2008 Housing 21 and the Department of Health's National End of Life Care Programme began a six-month service improvement project at three sites, focused on enabling terminally ill extra-care tenants to die at home where that was their wish. The project was evaluated over the same period using qualitative and quantitative approaches.

Objectives

The Department of Health *End of Life Care Strategy* was published in July 2008. The strategy acknowledged that the experience of death has changed profoundly with far less familiarity with death and dying than was the case a century ago, and with most deaths (58%) occurring in hospital following a period of chronic illness.

As the Commons health select committee inquiry on palliative care also noted four years ago, despite these trends, when questioned the majority of people state that they would prefer to die in their own homes. While some people have excellent end-of-life care, many do not. Too many people experience unnecessary pain and distress, are not treated with dignity and respect and do not die the "good death" that they would prefer. The national strategy addresses the need for high quality end-of-life care for everyone, wherever they may be.

The [United Kingdom's] national strategy addresses the need for high quality end-of-life care for everyone, wherever they may be.

It was against this background that the Housing 21 and NHS End of Life care team undertook the service improvement pilot project designed to enhance dignity and choice in end-of-life care in three extra-care housing settings in England. The specific objectives of the project were to:

- Enable terminally ill residents of extra-care housing to die at home if they chose to.

- Put in place processes to ascertain residents' preferences and to maximise the capacity of extra-care housing providers to support those choices.

- Develop an integrated approach in the community to accessing support for tenants, their families and carers and staff.

- Explore the challenges of providing end-of-life care in extra-care housing settings.

- Improve the skills and knowledge of staff.

- Develop high quality data monitoring tools and ensure good baseline data.

Findings

The project undertook in-depth work with the three extra-care sites, surveyed all 35 of the Housing 21 extra-care schemes (using a written questionnaire) and gathered data on recent deaths among tenants. Four key issues were identified across both the fieldwork sites and other data collections. These were:

- Promoting dignity and choice for older people and family carers.

- Support and training for staff.

- Extra care and its links to wider health and specialist resources.

- Commissioning and funding.

The views of extra-care tenants about end-of-life matters were as diverse as among any other population. While some were open in their views about death and clear about their own preferences about what they would like to happen at the end of their life, others were negative or avoided confronting the subject.

> *The wishes of [extra-care housing] tenants and of their families are not always the same and . . . [researchers] found that "in such cases it seemed relatively common for the family's wishes to take priority over those of the tenant."*

Responses to the questionnaire highlighted situations where dementia or other cognitive impairment had profound consequences in reducing or removing the ability of people to communicate their wishes.

It was particularly worrying that staff working in housing and in health often did not understand arrangements introduced by the Mental Capacity Act 2005. As the report notes, the provisions for the new Welfare Lasting Power of Attorney are especially relevant to end-of-life care since they allow for a person to be appointed to make health decisions on someone's behalf if they should lack the mental capacity to do so for themselves. Tenants of extra-care schemes were often similarly unaware that new arrangements extend Enduring Powers of Attorney beyond financial matters and into the territory of decisions about health interventions.

Information from the survey questionnaire indicated that tenants who were "least likely to have their wishes about end-of-life care either known about or met" were those who had not lived in the schemes for very long, and whom staff, there-fore, knew less well than established residents. People who had lived longest in extra-care schemes and whose deaths were ex-pected were more likely to die in their flat, while hospital deaths were more likely to be unexpected and to occur among more recent tenants. While deaths that occurred within an extra-care scheme were believed to have met the preferences of 75% of those people, this was true of only 20% of the deaths of tenants that occurred in hospitals.

The wishes of tenants and of their families are not always the same and the project found that "in such cases it seemed relatively common for the family's wishes to take priority over those of the tenant." This is a particularly important finding in the light of the personalization agenda set out in Putting People First and the emphasis on maximising control and self-determination.

Staff in extra-care housing have a potentially important role to play in helping residents to articulate their preferences about death and dying. At the outset of the project staff re-vealed the same discomfort about such subjects as many other people and would typically avoid such discussion, or worry that they were ill-equipped to support tenants in addressing difficult subjects. However, in the course of the evaluation staff reported becoming more confident in having these discussions, particularly after having attended training sessions.

While extra-care housing provides access to support for tenants, this is not equivalent to the level or intensity of support that might be available in a care home. Assumptions and misunderstandings about what a scheme can or cannot deliver can have negative consequences for sick and dying tenants. The study reported, for example, that in one scheme district nurses did not realise that staff were providing additional overnight support on a voluntary basis to support the night cover staff because a tenant was dying. Once they became aware of this, in a similar situation they would arrange for the Marie Curie overnight sitting service "as they would for other patients living in their own homes."

Sometimes inappropriate assumptions about what extra-care staff are able to do around complex caring tasks can create stress for staff who may not feel adequately equipped, and it can also be problematic if it means staff are acting outside Commission for Social Care Inspection regulations. Lack of knowledge and understanding of the role of extra-care housing could lead hospital staff to make inappropriate judgements about whether a person could return to a housing scheme or should enter a nursing home. The evaluation found that poor partnership working between the acute and community health sectors meant that such judgements could be made without involvement of scheme managers, or discussion with the older person about their wishes.

Analysis

People are moving into extra-care housing with higher levels of need (including dementia) and at more advanced years. At the same time, the emphasis on increasing personalisation in health and social care—with greater support for people to exercise choice and control—and the personalised focus of the

Terms Used in the United Kingdom for a Variety of Living Situations for the Elderly

- *Extra-Care Housing.* In this situation, people live in their own homes or apartments. They can mostly manage taking care of themselves. A site manager and care staff provide assistance when needed, and residents often receive help with meals, bathing, or other difficult-to-manage activities. In the United States, this might be termed "assisted living."

- *Care Home.* A care home is a large residential facility. Residents have their own rooms, but all live under the same roof. A full-time staff provides for most of the needs of the clients, including limited nursing. In a care home, a resident receives more help than in extra-care housing, but less than in a nursing home.

- *Nursing Home.* As in the United States, a nursing home is a facility that provides all the services a resident needs, including twenty-four-hour staff and nursing services. People living in nursing homes are not so sick that they need hospital care, but they do need medical attention on a daily or regular basis. They are not able to provide the most basic kinds of care for themselves.

Compiled by the editor.

End of Life Care Strategy are resulting in a significant challenge for extra-care schemes to make these principles a reality.

The study identifies particular challenges where the housing and extra-care elements of a scheme are managed or provided by different organisations. Both the housing and the extra-care agencies need to be fully engaged in understanding the implications of personalising the support they offer. Good quality support and end-of-life care require people to work together across professional and organisational boundaries. As the report points out, achieving what a tenant wants at the end of their life requires prior knowledge and understanding of those aspirations, as well as of what the extra-care scheme is able to support and provide.

Helping people to have a good death is an aspiration that all health and care services should support.

Many of the recommendations offered by the report are simple and straightforward and include: focusing on ensuring clarity about different roles and responsibilities; taking opportunities to raise awareness about the importance of death and dying; reviewing policies and procedures to incorporate end-of-life care issues; and supporting skills development and training for extra-care housing staff.

Even in the course of this brief and small-scale project it was evident that change could be achieved. During the evaluation it became more normal for staff to talk and think about end-of-life care. Staff also became more expert in identifying signs that someone was approaching the end of their life and to know how to respond. The developing engagement of staff also meant that there was more interaction with health and care staff and discussion about how extra-care schemes could support end-of-life care.

As Jeremy Porteus, Department of Health national programme lead, observes in the foreword to the report: "It is hard to think of a more personalised issue than how we die," and as the *End-of-Life Care Strategy* makes clear, helping people to have a good death is an aspiration that all health and care services should support. This has enormous implications for hospitals, care homes and hospices, but the role of the community and of extra-care housing within that will be increasingly important in supporting people to die at home with dignity.

Melanie Henwood is an independent health and social care consultant.

In Germany, Television Provides Information About Death and Dying

Charles Hawley

In the following viewpoint, Charles Hawley reports on the 2007 establishment of a twenty-fours-hours-a-day, seven-days-a-week German television channel devoted entirely to the subject of death and dying. Called EosTV, the station's programming will be aimed at Germany's rapidly aging population and will also include video obituaries. The programming will be largely informational and include how to select a retirement home, how to choose a funeral director, and documentaries about graveyards. Hawley is a writer for the German magazine Spiegel.

As you read, consider the following questions:

1. How many people does Wolf Tilmann Schneider think are affected by Germany's eight hundred thousand deaths in 2006?
2. In what did Germany's funeral homes note a rise?
3. Where are some of the cemeteries Schneider hopes to feature in documentaries?

There are shows for cooking, relationships, weddings and property—why not for dying? A new TV channel in Germany plans to rectify the omission with 24/7 digital death.

Charles Hawley, "Dead Air: New TV Channel Takes on Death and Dying," *Spiegel Online International*, June 22, 2007. Copyright © *Spiegel Online* 2007. Reproduced by permission.

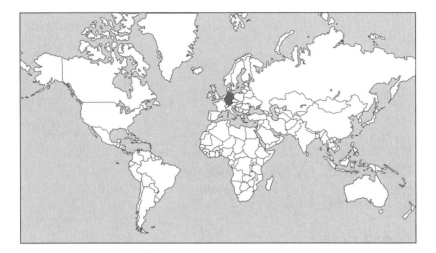

Cooking shows are a dime a dozen on television these days. Home improvement shows hit the big time in the 1990s. Property shows are huge in Britain. Relationships and weddings have likewise become popular prime-time fodder. But the one event that faces every human on Earth has never had its own television channel. Until now.

Starting this autumn [2007] in Germany, EosTV—a 24-hours-a-day, seven-days-a-week television channel devoted exclusively to aging, dying and mourning—will hit the airwaves. Viewers will be served up documentaries about cemeteries, shows about changing funeral culture, and helpful tips about finding a retirement home or nursing care. Should you be looking to install a stair lift in your home, EosTV will be the place to find information about that, too. Death and dying, in other words, right in your living room.

The one event that faces every human on Earth has never had its own television channel. Until now.

"Over 800,000 people died in Germany last year [2006]," Wolf Tilmann Schneider, the channel's founder, told *Spiegel Online.* "Multiply that by four and you have the rough number of people directly affected by those deaths. There are also 2.1 million people in Germany needing care in their old age. There are millions of people confronting the issues of getting older and dying."

Forest Cemeteries and Anonymous Burials

The show pairs television veteran Schneider with Germany's funeral home association and seeks to take advantage of the country's changing demographics. In 2006, Germany saw almost 150,000 more deaths than births, a continuation of a trend that has seen the country's population age dramatically in recent decades.

In addition, says Kerstin Gernig, spokeswoman for the National Association of Funeral Homes, there has also been a recent shift in the way people approach death and burial. More people are taking advantage of anonymous burials, for example. Forest cemeteries are likewise becoming more popular, as are Internet graveyards. And the church no longer plays such a large role in the death industry.

In 2006, Germany saw almost 150,000 more deaths than births, a continuation of a trend that has seen the country's population age dramatically in recent decades.

"We want to take a look at the changing nature of mourning and death in the Internet, pictures and movies," Gernig told *Spiegel Online* in reference to the new death channel.

The channel, which will cost less than €10 million [about $14 million USD] to launch, would also like to be a part of that trend. For years, Germany's funeral homes have noted a rise in the number of elderly people and their descendents looking to work with professional writers to document their lives and those of loved ones.

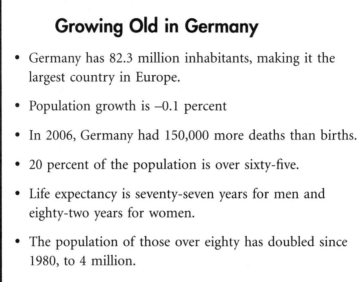

Growing Old in Germany

- Germany has 82.3 million inhabitants, making it the largest country in Europe.

- Population growth is –0.1 percent

- In 2006, Germany had 150,000 more deaths than births.

- 20 percent of the population is over sixty-five.

- Life expectancy is seventy-seven years for men and eighty-two years for women.

- The population of those over eighty has doubled since 1980, to 4 million.

- In 2003, German president Horst Köhler sent 4,210 birthday cards to those who reached their hundredth birthdays.

- More than eight hundred thousand people died in Germany in 2006.

- Germany's funeral association, representing 85 percent of the industry in that country, supports and backs EosTV.

Compiled by the editor.

Televised Obituaries

Working with the funeral home association—which represents some 85 percent of German undertakers—Schneider is hoping to provide families a video outlet for their mourning as well. Families can buy 30-second slots to create televised obituaries. For a €2,400 fee [about $3,583 USD], the spot will be aired

10 times on the death channel and will also be provided as video on the company's Web site and those of funeral homes.

"We are all the same. We all have the same life cycle and we all live and die," says Schneider. "That's where the idea came from that—just like an obituary one places with a newspaper—I wanted to give people the opportunity to do that on television."

Most of the programming, however, will be taken up by informational shows for the elderly. Those moving into their later years can watch the channel to inform themselves about life insurance, funeral insurance, home nursing services, and which companies are the best at installing stair lifts.

Program directors are even hoping to do shows on Germans' seeming unwillingness to donate their organs. The shows, Schneider hopes, will be sponsored by companies selling products to those entering their golden years.

Graveyard Documentaries

And of course, there will be entertainment programming. Schneider can barely contain himself when he talks about his own interest in cemeteries. "I realized recently," he says breathlessly, "that I really like going to the cemetery. And I've noticed that in Germany and in Europe people go to cemeteries not just to mourn, but also to enjoy the peace."

His idea? Documentaries on European cemeteries. What happens to bodies in Germany after their allotted cemetery time—as a rule, dead Germans stay in the ground for no longer than a generation—has expired? What about that beautiful graveyard in Paris? And then there's the cemetery in Berlin that was divided by the Berlin Wall. The list of potential topics, so says Schneider, is endless.

So too, he is hoping, is the target group. After all, he points out, hundreds of thousands of people die in Germany *each year*. And it's not just a German phenomenon. Indeed, before the first show has even been broadcast, EosTV—named for Eos, the Greek goddess of the dawn—is already planning to expand.

Schneider has begun the search for partners across Europe and in the United States. The response, he reports, has been quite lively.

Periodical Bibliography

The following articles have been selected to supplement the diverse views presented in this chapter.

Jane E. Brody	"In Cancer Therapy, There Is a Time to Treat and a Time to Let Go," *New York Times*, August 18, 2008.
Mike Ceaser	"Euthanasia in Legal Limbo in Colombia," *Lancet*, January 26, 2008.
Adrian Dabscheck	"Focus on Easing Pain," *Age* (Australia), June 25, 2008.
Brian Donnelly	"Calls for Terminally-Ill Patients to Have Greater Choice of Where to Die," *Herald* (Scotland), April 29, 2009.
Simon Gaskell	"Preparation for Death Will Help Your Loved Ones," *Evening Chronicle* (England), November 30, 2009.
Róisín Ingle	"Living and Dying with Dignity," *Irish Times*, December 13, 2008.
Len Kelly et al.	"Palliative Care of First Nations People: A Qualitative Study of Bereaved Family Members," *Canadian Family Physician*, April 2009.
Kay Lazar	"Terminally Ill Patients Delay Talk of Hospice; Study Finds Many Have Unrealistic Outlook," *Boston Globe*, May 26, 2009.
Pulse	"Debate: Should GPs Play a Role in Assisting a Patient's Death?" November 11, 2009.
Margaret Somerville	"Doctors Should Kill the Pain, Not the Patient: Euthanasia Debate Should Not Be Confused with the Need for Pain-Relief Management," *Ottawa Citizen*, July 28, 2009.
Jennifer Yeo and Madan Mohan	"Right to Die—or License to Kill?" *Straits Times* (Singapore), December 24, 2008.

GLOBALVIEWPOINTS

CHAPTER 3

Death, Dying, and Religion

Religion Influences Attitudes Toward Death Worldwide

Anna Orońska

In the following viewpoint, Anna Orońska of the Palliative Care Center in Wroclaw, Poland, discusses the importance of religion in preserving the dignity of the dying. She describes death rituals of Judaism, Islam, Hinduism, and Buddhism. She argues that the most important rule of palliative care is that the caregiver should show respect for the dying person's religious beliefs by knowing what those beliefs and customs are and by following them.

As you read, consider the following questions:

1. What are the Chevra Kadisha, according to the author?
2. How does Orońska say a dying Muslim should be placed in bed?
3. Why is an endless prolonging of life pointless for Buddhists, according to the author?

The attitude to death is the most crucial issue of religious and philosophical systems.

"From the perspective of the world religions dying is a sacred craft, an authentic ritual, the last chance giving us the possibility to discover the meaning and purpose of life" [according to writer P.K. Kramer].

Anna Orońska, "The Dignity of a Dying Human in Different Religions of the World," *Advances in Palliative Medicine*, vol. 8, no. 2, November 2, 2009, pp. 63–66. Copyright © 2009 by Via Medica. Reproduced by permission.

This definition clearly suggests that the concept of dying in the light of religion brings the acceptance of the dignity of a dying human being.

The meaning of death bears the testimony to the dignity of a dying person—the circumstances of death can help in understanding this dignity by the dying and their surroundings, but cannot alter the fact that the most difficult death can be a dignified death (for example death in a concentration camp). What decides about the dignity of dying is not the external, but the spiritual aspect.

The most important assumption of palliative care is the respect for religious beliefs and patients' confessions.

Certainly, the rituals of different religions underline this dignity in various ways. A very significant exponent of respect for the dignity of the dying is constituted by the rituals connected with the funeral and experiencing the mourning. Thus, profanation of the dead body is treated as one of the most hideous crimes.

All the traditional religions treat death as a way of transformation as opposed to the contemporary lay culture, which treats death as a threat to life arousing anxiety and as destruction, although it also emphasizes the right to a "dignified death", understanding it rather more as creating proper external conditions (lack of pain, suffering, disability) and in some cases accepting the possibility of euthanasia. Let us analyse the approach to death in 4 most prominent world religions: Judaism, Islam, Hinduism and Buddhism.

This issue has more than only a theoretical meaning. Modern societies are getting more and more multicultural and multi-confessional. The most important assumption of palliative care is the respect for religious beliefs and patients' confessions.

The proof of respecting the dignity of a dying human, even if it differs from our beliefs and customs, is providing spiritual care according to patients' needs, if possible also the ritual connected with dying and not violating their religious restrictions.

Jewish Death Rituals

The approach to death in Judaism was changing throughout centuries. The Bible did not exactly give any precise view on life after death. There were various images:

- return to ancestors;

- return to God;

- staying in Sheol;

- death as a consequence of the sin of Adam and Eve, but also one's individual sin.

The belief in resurrection appeared quite late in 5th–3rd century B.C. The Torah does not describe any particular rituals connected with death. A negative attitude to a dead human body is characteristic (touching a dead body caused ritual impurity). However, the obligation to bury the body was very important, in times close to the New Testament it was connected with a specific ritual that required anointment with fragrant oils, wrapping the body in cloth and putting into the grave, which was often a cave cut in the rock.

Nowadays in the majority of Jewish communities there are organizations taking care of the dead, which are called Chevra Kadisha (the "holy society"). A contemporary Jew is also more concentrated on living in accordance with the commandments and performing good deeds than on engaging himself in a profound theology of life after death.

An important element to secure dignity to a dying person is the presence of close relatives and a prayer for the dying.

Jewish Respect for Life

The respect for life following the Mosaic laws is absolute and complete. The value of human life does not alter when s/he suffers from an incurable, fatal disease. Until the breathing and brain function does . . . stop, it is not allowed to do anything that could accelerate death. It is prohibited to touch the man in his agony, to neaten his pillow or close his eyelids, because there is a threat that the smallest movement could shorten his life. However, it does not mean that one's life should be prolonged at any cost. Obviously, any direct action aiming at shortening one's life is forbidden.

Most rabbis claim that the Talmud law allows to resign from any action that is only the case of "therapeutic ferocity". It is permitted to administer painkillers in order to relieve or alleviate pain.

But there are still a few rabbis who take the position that every human life has to be prolonged at any cost.

After death the body should not be left without care, the staff (of any other confession) cannot touch the body. The activities such as closing the eyes, cleaning or dressing the body are performed by the son or the closest family. The funeral should take place within 24 hours. . . .

Islamic Customs

According to the Koran, God gives life and death. Life deserves the highest respect, because it comes from God, but death is not evil. . . .

Similarly, the dignity of a human being comes from God.

Human body—alive or dead—should be treated with respect, as the work of the Creator. Human body does not belong to the man—it belongs to God, who will point at it on the Judgement day. The belief in resurrection is one of the basic dogmas of Islam.

As everything is the creation of God, the illness but also medicines are treated as such. The doctor performs the will of

God. If God wants the death of his worshipper, this moment should not be accelerated or postponed. Neither euthanatic practices nor "therapeutic ferocity" are accepted. It is confirmed by the Islamic Code of Medical Ethics from 1981.

> [The] human body—alive or dead—should be treated with respect, as the work of the Creator.

The doctor is not allowed to perform any procedures that may shorten life. He is also not allowed to stop any procedures that may give any chance of restoring a patient's health. A patient's will is of no great importance. The life-saving procedures should not prolong the process of dying.

As it comes to the painkillers, Islam believers are not allowed to take any addictive agents (including alcohol and drugs). Yet, when the pain exceeds the tolerable level it is permitted to administer morphine. A dying person should be laid with his face toward Mecca. Nobody considered "impure" (e.g. a woman with menstrual bleeding) should stay in the same room. A dying person or the relatives say the proper Koran suras and the basic Islam credo: "There is no God but Allah, and Muhammad is his Prophet".

One closes the eyes of the deceased, ties his legs, cleans the body and anoints it with fragrant oils (family; the members of staff have to wear gloves). The autopsy is prohibited. The burial should take place within 24 hours. . . .

Hindu Death Ritual

Death in Hinduism is a natural and inevitable thing, yet it is not authentic—it is not the end of life. . . .

Death is the end of a certain phase—life after death is just different. The belief in reincarnation (transmigration) is characteristic of Hinduism—at the moment of death our physical flesh leaves us and the soul (jiva) returns to the stage of temporary happiness, and then is reborn in a new physical flesh

Religion and Spirituality Influence End-of-Life Communication

Cross-cultural communication becomes especially important when dealing with end-of-life issues. For example, decision making might be very difficult for a patient who believes that someone else should make decisions about issues such as withholding resuscitation efforts. In many cultures, decision-making power for family members is given to the member of highest status, which may be the eldest male.

[Researchers have] . . . identified issues related to end-of-life care that may be influenced by cultural beliefs and should be taken into account by health care professionals:

- Religion and spirituality should be acknowledged and respected.

- An increased desire for futile care at the end of life may exist, and possibly a lack of interest in hospice services, because of an underlying concern that not all the best options are being offered.

- People in many cultures believe that informing the patient of a terminal diagnosis may hasten death. Thus, an agreement needs to be reached between the physician and the patient and patient's family on withholding a terminal diagnosis. Questions to ask a patient include: "How much do you want to know about your illness?" or "Do you prefer that I discuss (or not discuss) your diagnosis with you or with your family?"

Dixie Dennis, Living, Dying, Grieving. *Sudbury, MA: Jones and Bartlett Publishers, 2009, p. 81.*

at the time and in the way determined by karma. The ultimate goal is liberating oneself from the circle of death and rebirth and the ultimate unification with Brahman—the Absolute Reality. The preparation for death, especially in case of monks, is called moksha—spiritual death that allows to avoid further incarnations and unify with the Absolute.

Euthanasia and aided suicide are forbidden, because the aim of a man in the present life is to deserve a better "karma" in the future life. The acceptable form of the suicide is self-starvation or self-suffocation by means of holding breath, used by the monks in order to achieve nirvana. Hinduism does not support artificial prolonging of life.

Before death, the son or relatives should pour into the dying person's mouth water taken—if it is possible—from the Ganges river. It relieves thirst and at the same time guarantees that the dying person will receive the Ganges blessing. The surrounding sings pious songs and Vedic mantras which bring solace. . . .

If there is a monk present—he recites mantras and states death.

The body after cleaning and anointment is burnt at the stake in a special ritual. However, it is worth noticing, that the notion of "dignity" practically differs from our European idea. People from the lower caste, considered as those with "bad karma"—can deserve through their suffering a better karma in the next incarnation. Maybe that is the reason why nobody cares about a poor Hindu dying in the street. The idea of the "dignity of a dying human" was introduced on this ground by Mother Teresa of Calcutta and is still implemented by her spiritual daughters—the missionaries of love. For many of us this way of emphasizing the dignity of a dying human became an inspiration for work in palliative care.

Buddhist Beliefs About Death

Nirvana—is the land without death; what is left when illusions, ignorance, desire and attachment disappear.

One cannot understand it, it is a mystical experience. Entering nirvana while living denies the power of death.

The Buddhist doctrine of rebirth (unlike the Hindu one) does not cover the belief in soul which can be reborn in further incarnations. What is reborn is rather the state of consciousness.

One can imagine the reincarnation in Hinduism as successive beads on a string, but this process in the Buddhist doctrine resembles rather the way of building the tower of blocks.

The first moment—the thought of future life will be born as a consequence of the last moment—the thought of the present life.

Therefore, it is important that the dying takes place with full consciousness, with the mind clear and calm.

The dying person should be surrounded by friends, family, monks reading sutras and repeating mantras which help the dying one to achieve a serene state of spirit. The contemporary Buddhist monks advise using the palliative medicine procedures, including the use of painkillers that do not disturb the consciousness but secure tranquil physical as well as spiritual leaving.

The destruction of the body through a suicide or euthanasia does not make sense. It causes that the spirit leaves in an unfavourable atmosphere and in the future it will carry bad marks of this action (bad karma). Apart from that, if you break the suffering, it will continue in the next incarnation, until it is completed.

Since for a Buddhist the death does not mean a defeat, an endless prolonging of life is pointless. If there is no chance for recovery, any attempts of artificial life prolonging should be abandoned. At this very moment the man does not need any further medical treatment, but rather moral and spiritual support which will allow him to die in peace and dignity.

After death the body should not be left alone. Near the head of the deceased one puts the vase with flowers (representing Buddha); after 3 days the body is burnt.

Respecting the Dead

In the above paper we discussed the approach to death in 4 great world religions: Judaism, Islam, Hinduism and Buddhism. The respect for death and the will to make it dignified is characteristic of each of those religions. All of those religious systems are also marked with high respect for life—suicide (although in practice it looks a bit different in case of Islam and Hinduism) and euthanasia are unacceptable. Similarly—except for a small fraction of super-Orthodox Jews—the idea of the "persistent therapy" is wrong.

Yet one should remember that each of these 4 religions has numerous factions that differ in their approach even to the most fundamental issues connected with life and death. Apart from that—everywhere practice does not always correspond to the beautiful ideals which are the basis of a particular religion.

In this work we avoided any comparisons to Christianity, but everyone can find here numerous similarities and differences.

The respect for death and the will to make it dignified is characteristic of [Judaism, Islam, Hinduism, and Buddhism].

The basic rule of palliative care, important especially in multicultural societies of Western Europe or America, is respect for a patient's beliefs and religious convictions.

It is significant to know them in order not to violate the dignity of a dying human being. It should be also noticed that in Poland appears (following the Western idea) the tendency to introduce Buddhist meditation techniques together with the general Buddhist philosophy concerning the care of an ill person who is suffering and dying.

For every Christian patient this could be dangerous, because it hinders the opening for the transcendent God. Each and every religion has valuable elements of a dignified experiencing of dying and death itself—but only the man who had professed this religion before is able to use it to the greatest extent.

In the United States, Many Religious and Cultural Traditions Influence Death Rituals

Sandra L. Lobar, JoAnne M. Youngblut, and Dorothy Brooten

In the following viewpoint, Sandra L. Lobar, JoAnne M. Youngblut, and Dorothy Brooten describe beliefs, ceremonies, and rituals surrounding the death of a loved one in different cultures. They begin with discussing Mexican American, Cuban American, and Puerto Rican customs. Next, they turn to Caribbean practices, stating that these beliefs are a blend of Catholicism and African or indigenous folk religion. Also discussed are African American and Asian customs. They conclude with a discussion of Jewish, Christian, and Islamic practices. Lobar, Youngblut, and Brooten are professors in the School of Nursing at Florida International University.

As you read, consider the following questions:

1. Why do Mexicans have more understanding and acceptance of death, according to the authors?
2. How is the body of a Hindu treated after death, according to the authors?
3. What themes emerge in Chinese cultural responses to death and dying, according to the authors?

Sandra L. Lobar, JoAnne M. Youngblut, and Dorothy Brooten, "Cross-Cultural Beliefs, Ceremonies, and Rituals Surrounding the Death of a Loved One," *Pediatric Nursing*, vol. 32, no. 1, January–February 2006, pp. 44–50. Copyright © 2006 Anthony J. Jannetti, Inc. Reprinted with permission of the publisher, Jannetti Publications, Inc.

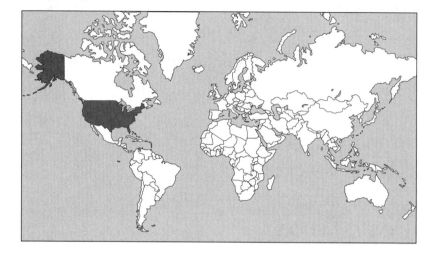

Researchers have found greater outward expression of grief and more physiologic reactions among Mexican American college students compared to Anglo college students and greater grief intensity among Latinos from Puerto Rico who experienced a sudden unexpected death than other Latinos and Anglos. However, [they] found no differences in bereavement for white, black, and Hispanic adult children whose parent died from cancer. [Other researchers] identified similarities during the period preceding the death in case studies of a Mexican American family, a Cuban American family, and a Puerto Rican family experiencing the death of a family member, including the caregiver's not wanting to burden or impose on family; experiencing depressive symptoms; and relying on faith, hope, and prayer to cope with the impending death.

In another case study report, [J.] Rivera-Andino and [L.] Lopez reported that Hispanics believe it is detrimental to patients to let them know about the seriousness of the illness in order to spare them unnecessary pain and that it is the family's obligation to take over control of the situation. African Americans may hold mistrust of the health care system, especially regarding advanced directives and end-of-life care, and both

Mexican Americans and African Americans verbalize a preference for decision making as a family.

Latino and Caribbean Death Rituals

Latino death rituals are described as heavily influenced by Catholic beliefs where spirituality is very important and there is a continuing relationship between the living and the dead through prayer and visits to the grave. Grief is expressed by crying openly where women may wail loudly but men may act according to "machismo" where there is a belief that men should act strong and not show overt emotion. There is preference for burial rather than cremation, novenas for 9 days, mass for the deceased during the first year and then yearly, family gatherings with food (like a wake), and lighting candles.

Descendents from Caribbean nations and Mexico may practice a blend of Catholicism and African or indigenous folk medicine known as Santería in Cuba, Espiritismo in Puerto Rico, or voodoo in other Caribbean nations, and Curanderismo in Mexico. Santería death rituals are governed by the saints (orishas) as told by the santero (a clergy or holy man) and often include animal sacrifice. [B.] Younoszai asserts that Mexicans have more understanding and acceptance of death because their country is primarily rural, poor, religious, and very young on average. Death is portrayed in Mexican statues, art, literature, and history, and Mexican children are socialized early to accept death, giving Mexicans a "cultural familiarity with death." Mexicans and other Latinos celebrate "Día de los Muertos" (Day of the Dead) to remember and honor the dead.

African American and Asian Responses to Death

Death rituals for black Americans vary widely, perhaps because of the diversity in religious affiliations, geographic region, education, and economics. Researchers suggest that emotional expression varies, with some black Americans crying and wailing while others are silent and stoic. [H.L.] Perry describes large gatherings and an expressed obligation to pay respects to the deceased as common. Southern and rural blacks may maintain the custom of having the corpse at the house for the evening before the funeral. Friends and family gather at the house to help out where they can. Church "nurses" help family members to view the body. Women "flower girls" escort the casket with the pallbearers and pay special attention to the family. Strong religious beliefs—seeing the death as a reflection of God's will or plans, believing the deceased is in God's hands, and being reunited in heaven after death—help many black Americans to grieve while maintaining a connection with the deceased. Bereaved African Americans are more likely to seek help from clergy than health care professionals. For Baptists, heaven is a place where the redeemed go to and it is described as filled, a beautiful place, and there is belief in resurrection.

Bereaved African Americans are more likely to seek help from clergy than health care professionals.

In the Asian culture, the death of an infant or child is deeply mourned. Family members may wear white clothing or headbands for a period of time. Traditional elaborate funeral ceremonies were the norm for marking the soul's passing to the afterlife. Sadness and grief may be expressed as somatic complaints, since mental illness is often considered a disgrace to the family. Buddhist belief uses death as an opportunity for improvement in the next life. To enter death in a positive state of mind and surrounded by monks and family helps the deceased to become reborn on a higher level. Local family customs require a display of grief, wearing of traditional white cloth, openly showing grief, and even wailing at times. The body should be handled in a worthy and respectful way. Hinduism is unique as a religion because its roots do not spring from [a] single scripture, founder, or sacred place but is seen as more of an umbrella term to describe a set of philosophies, cultures, and way of life. However, the approach to death is fairly uniform because the belief in the laws of karma and reincarnation suggests that each birth is linked to actions taken in previous births, and that births and deaths are part of a cycle that each person is seeking to transcend through the accumulation of good Karmas (actions) ultimately leading to liberation of the soul.

When a Hindu dies, the body is bathed, massaged in oils, dressed in new clothes, then cremated before the next sunrise to facilitate the soul's transition from this world to the next. Rituals are conducted for 10 days while the deceased member's soul watches over the family. On the 11th day, the soul releases its attachment to the former life.

[A.G.] Yick and [R.] Gupta conducted multiple focus groups with Chinese participants to describe Chinese Americans' beliefs and practices regarding death and dying. They suggested that many of the current descriptions of cultural bereavement practices are portrayed in a static manner and noted that it is important to understand the evolving nature of culture over time and based on history. Cultural dimensions of death, dying, and bereavement in the Chinese culture included the following themes: (a) Saving Face (the more people who cry for the deceased, the more the person was loved), (b) Filial Piety (duty to one's relative), and (c) Invoking Luck, Blessing, and Fortune (belief in life, afterlife, and presence of spirit).

[In Jewish custom], a black ribbon or torn clothing symbolizing mourning or grief is worn by mourners.

Jewish, Christian, and Islamic Practices

Death rituals for other groups identified by religious belief such as Judaism have also been described. There are several

Paying Last Respects Across Cultures

Death doesn't stop there. It beats at the door of Christians and Jews, Muslims and Buddhists. It's just around the corner for everybody.

If you have friends and coworkers of different faiths and cultures, you might someday have to console them for a loved one's loss—but may not know how.

Most people know their own faith's funeral customs. But since death is a sensitive issue, it's easy to step into a cultural minefield. You don't want to bring a baked ham to a grieving Jewish family or tell jokes at a subdued Muslim funeral, for example, even if you grew up in a culture that finds pork products and conviviality at funerals perfectly OK.

Funeral directors emphasize that grieving families will appreciate any gesture you make to console them, even if you're hazy on the theological nuances. . . .

If the bereaved's culture is unfamiliar, though, stay on the safe side by telling the mourners you are sorry for their loss, dressing conservatively for the wake or service and being respectful of the family's traditions.

> *Pam DeFiglio,*
> *"Paying Your Last Respects: How to Avoid Cross-Cultural*
> *Blunders While Consoling Friends of Other Faiths,"*
> Daily Herald, *November 2, 2006.*

major groups within Judaism and the interpretation of Jewish law and practice may allow for wide variation in rituals. Funerals are generally performed as soon after death as possible because there is a belief that the soul begins a return to heaven immediately after death. There is also a belief that the body is a holy repository of the soul and should be treated and cared for with respect. A black ribbon or torn clothing symbolizing mourning or grief is worn by mourners. Shivah is the process of receiving guests during the grieving process. Families are cared for by their friends and the religious community while they contemplate their loss. Mourners may stay seated on low stools, mirrors may be covered, and mourners may perform only minimal amounts of grooming and/or bathing. Families may not place a headstone at the gravesite until the first year anniversary of the death coinciding with the end of the traditional year of mourning. There is a daily recitation of the Kaddish, a life-affirming mourning prayer by mourners. It is important to understand the religious beliefs often change and observant people may become more or less observant when death occurs or may wish to break with tradition when faced with death.

In addition to Judaism and Christianity, Islam is a third major monotheistic religion that guides death practices. At the time of death it is believed that the soul is exposed to God. There is a belief about afterlife, and Islam dictates that the purpose of the worldly life is to prepare for the eternal life. The dying patient should be positioned facing Mecca, the room is perfumed, and anyone who is unclean should leave the room. Passages for the Quran are read to the dying patient. Organ donation is permissible with family permission when a patient is determined to be brain dead. Family members prepare the body for burial following the pronouncement of death. Muslim culture does not encourage wailing but crying is permissible. Personal prayers are recited while standing but prayers from the Quran may not be recited near the corpse. Women are traditionally prohibited from visiting cemeteries.

In Thailand, Buddhist Beliefs About Karma Affect End-of-Life Care

Kittikorn Nilmanat and Annette F. Street

In the following viewpoint, Kittikorn Nilmanat and Annette F. Street recount their study of the care given by four Thai families who were caring for people dying from AIDS. The families and those who were dying were Buddhist, and the Buddhist concept of karma—especially the popular understanding of karma as "bad luck as punishment for previously committed sin"—played a large role in the care given. Nilmanat is a member of the Faculty of Nursing, Prince of Songkla University, Thailand. Street is professor of Cancer and Palliative Care Studies at La Trobe University and director of Austin Health Clinical School of Nursing at La Trobe University—Bundoora, Victoria, Australia. This information is not a tool for self-diagnosis or a substitute for professional care.

As you read, consider the following questions:

1. How was the fact that the individuals were dying from AIDS interpreted in terms of karma?

2. What are the two purposes of the religious rite known as *Jan Nean Are Yu*?

3. How is suicide viewed in terms of karma?

Kittikorn Nilmanat and Annette F. Street, "Karmic Quest: Thai Family Caregivers Promoting a Peaceful Death for People with AIDS," *Contemporary Nurse*, vol. 27, no. 1, December 2007, pp. 94–102. Copyright © 2007 eContent Management Pty Ltd. Reproduced by permission.

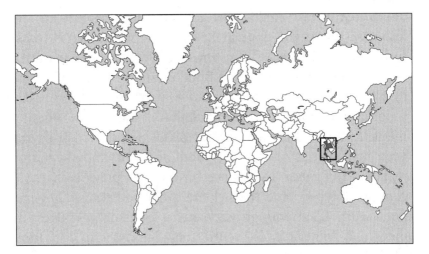

Introduction

Issues related to spiritual distress and spirituality among people with HIV/AIDS are common, as AIDS threatens the integrity of not only the patients but also their families. A diagnosis of AIDS often leads persons to a quest for meaning in their experience. . . . Feelings of anger, loss, uncertainty, vulnerability, guilt, shame, despair and hopelessness are common experiences in living with AIDS. . . .

In Thailand, a large proportion of the population has been affected by AIDS, either directly or indirectly, since the first case was reported in 1984. It was estimated that in 2005 the cumulative number of people with HIV [was] about 1,092,327, and 508,300 people with HIV/AIDS required health care services (Department of Epidemiology Ministry of Public Health 2005). The majority of people have little or no access to treatment; as a consequence, AIDS remains a fatal disease for most Thai people, and sufferers are often cared for by their own families at home. . . .

As 94.5% of the population in Thailand is Buddhist, the Buddhist doctrine has framed conceptions of life, suffering and death in Thai society. Although Philosophical Buddhism constructs the doctrine of Karma (or kamma in Pali), this sophisticated form is highly abstract and difficult to understand and practice. At the popular level, the term 'karma' is transformed to 'bad luck as punishment for previously committed sin'. . . . In everyday life, Thai Buddhists use the law of karma to interpret their present existence, particularly their social status, as the result of an accumulation of merit (*bun*) and demerit (*baab*). Wealthy and healthy people are viewed as having been meritorious or morally good, and can enjoy spending their fund of merit accumulated from their previous lives. In contrast, the poor and the sick are suffering because they had not accumulated enough good merit in their past lives. As merit and demerit is the central popular concern . . ., most Thai Buddhists perform merit making with the belief that it will improve their meritorious status and secure a successful reincarnation. . . .

This paper reports the constructions of karma by four Thai family caregivers living with a dying person with AIDS in Southern Thailand. These four families form a subset of a larger ethnographic case study exploring the experiences of families living with a relative with AIDS. Their stories were investigated further because karma was a shared dominant theme in their experience. Karma shaped and transformed their journeying towards death: a death that is also the beginning of the next cycle of reincarnation for a person with AIDS and a reconstruction of life for the families. In this paper, we explore how families make sense of their experiences of caring for their loved one with terminal AIDS and how they mobilise the religious resources and spiritual faith to promote a peaceful death for their loved one. . . .

Findings

Illness stories being told by families were not only stories of a search for cure . . .; they were also stories of lives that had been thrown into chaos by AIDS. . . . These families searched for alternative ways of living with illness and the immanent death of their loved one. The family members mobilised religious resources to make sense of suffering and as a means for perseverance. Families established a new connection of self to their experiences. The 'calm and peaceful' death that is described in the palliative care literature equated with their desire for the Buddhist philosophy of a harmonious death.

Karma as the Transformation of Suffering. Participants and family members looked for another frame of reference in order to explain and relieve their suffering. Families reasoned that their and the participant's suffering was their karma. These families used the notion of karma to make sense of their experiences and as a source of their moral and spiritual strength and comfort. This understanding of AIDS as fate or karma is evident in the following account:

> I have compassion on her. She is a diligent person. She has supported her brother and me to study and gave some of her income to our mother. Her life has been difficult for a long time.... and she has to receive karma like this.... [going to cry] ... Since it already happened, we have to take this karma ... [sobs] ... She realises this, too. She knows that her merit has been made up to this level ... [cry] ... (Wan's sister, informant)

Here moral judgments about the good in this life are weighed against a presupposed level of bad deeds from a previous life. The family accepted her karmic interpretation and transformed AIDS from a medical disease into a karmic disease. Notably, the medical definition of AIDS as a sexually transmitted disease was not mentioned in their everyday lives. Instead, families linked being sick with AIDS to their belief in karma. According to informants, a person who was born with merit would not suffer from illness, while a person with AIDS had been born with bad karma from a previous life, or had committed bad deeds [in] their current life. As a consequence of bad karma, families concluded, the participants suffered AIDS in this life.

In addition, these women interpreted their own suffering as the consequence of their karma. Ratree talked about the way she used karma to overcome her suffering from keeping her son's AIDS diagnosis secret:

> I realise that since our life is determined to be in this way, we have to accept our karma. We don't know how to do, so we have to accept it. I told my son that we both had to understand that I could not talk with other relatives about this thing. Nowadays, I feel uncomfortable to talk to others. They also became estranged. . . . [sigh] . . . I have to let it go. Whatever my merit has been made up to which level, I will let it go as it should be . . . because I don't know what to do too . . . Whatever will be, will be.

Notably, the medical definition of AIDS as a sexually transmitted disease was not mentioned in their everyday lives. Instead, families linked being sick with AIDS to their belief in karma.

Ratree assumed that her suffering stemmed from the desire to maintain her social relationships. Although Ratree needed help and support from others, she could not ask for help because her son had an 'unspeakable' disease. In order to alleviate this suffering, Ratree relied on her belief in karma to accept limitations and see the cause of the situation as a result of their own actions in a former life. As a consequence, she was able to let go of her negative feelings towards others and feel calm.

In addition, families usually tied their anticipated grief into their belief in karma. As Klub suggested, 'It is our karma. We received the command that our lives should end at a certain time.' These women were aware of the impermanence of life. They came to accept that death is inevitable and part of life. Families were therefore able to endure the suffering of anticipatory grief and loss. Religious faith also enabled families to plan for their future and for the next life of their loved one.

Karmic Quest: A Spiritual Journey. As the families believed that the lives of their loved ones were predetermined by karma, they attempted to compensate for this poor karma status by accumulating merit for them. Families performed religious rites and care at the end of life to promote a calm and peaceful death and improve the status of the dying person in the next life.

Helping the Participants Search for a Meaning and Purpose of Life. When the participants faced imminent death, their families helped them to clarify the meaning and the purpose of living. Here again, karmic belief was used to make sense of living and dying.

San was in the terminal AIDS stage. One week before San died, she suffered from pain and diarrhoea. As a consequence of this, San refused meals and medicines, although her family attempted to provide liquid foods and medicines in solution forms for her. Tan, the mother of San, explained:

> I told her that 'You should take it. If we have good merit, we will survive. It depends on our merit and karma. For this thing [living], if we have merit, we will be fine. But if it is time to go, we don't know what to do. Let it be in our merit and karma.' I told her like this.

Balancing Acts of Merit and Demerit. When San had hematamesis and a bloody stool, the family interpreted this situation as warning signs of her imminent death. The monks were called to perform the merit-making activities of *Jan Nean Are Yu* for her at home. In this activity the monks pour water on the hands of the dying person. Tan, her mother, spoke of this experience:

I invited a monk to do *Jan Nean Are Yu* for her. It aimed to make merit for her. We did it while she could hear and her eyes could see. If it works, she will be better. If not, she will die. If she is going to die soon, at least she can hear chants before she dies.

San's sister elaborated further on the meaning of this religious rite for the family:

Because she could not go to *Wai* [pay respect to the] monks there [at the temple]. So we invited them [monks] to visit her here. Then she could pay respect 'Wai' monks. If she passes away, she will see a light . . . Something like this . . . Thai people do like this . . .

The religious ceremony *Jan Nean Are Yu* was conducted with two purposes. The family still hoped that this meritorious activity would help the person to get better. However, the family knew that the prospect of recovery was weak. As San's stepfather stated, 'I told you that she has no return. She just waits for time when the messengers come to take her.' Therefore, this religious rite served the second purpose: to cultivate merit for the next life of San. In this sense, the family expected to transfer their merit to San in order to ensure her a better rebirth in the next world. Although families accepted the imminent death, they maintained spiritual hope.

Furthermore, since it is traditionally believed that the state of mind of the dying person at the moment of death influences the transitional state between each life form . . . , families believed that listening to the chants of the monks would direct the mind of their loved one to the Buddha. It is also believed that the monks' meritorious status makes dying people immune to the dangers of death. In this sense a monk acts as a spiritual healer for restitution from suffering in this life and as mediator between death and rebirth of the dying people. . . . As a consequence of this, the family believed that the monks took the *winjan* (soul) of San to heaven ('She will see the light').

In addition, to ensure balance of her merit and demerit before San died, the family also stopped her doing anything that might cause her demerits. San had thought of committing suicide several times. However, her family told her not to do this because it would be bad karma for her next life. Tan explained:

> It is like if she hangs herself in this life, she will do it again in the next life. It is said that a person, who hangs oneself, will do it again and again for 3 lives ... You see, as a monk taught us whatever we do in this life, we will receive that Karma in the next lives. I said to her, 'Let it go as it should be. Do not make [bad] Karma. Let you die with illness. Let it be natural death.' Let it be in her Karma.

In Traditional Buddhist societies, committing suicide is classified as a great demerit activity. The families believed that life did not end with physical death, but that there were other lives after this that could be influenced. They also believed that committing suicide would influence the forms of life after death. Tan was worried that if San had committed this demerit act, she would not escape from Karma or suffering in the next three lives. In this sense, the family expected that by suffering in this life, San would be freed from suffering in the next.

In addition, to ensure balance of her merit and demerit before San died, the family also stopped her doing anything that might cause her demerits.

Preparing the State of Mind of the Dying. To overcome karma and instill hope for a better life in the next world, several religious and spiritual activities were performed and practiced during the last minutes when the person was dying and after they had passed away. According to [M.J.] Eshleman (1992), when death is approaching, Buddhists attach great importance to the person's state of mind, which should be calm and clear. This peaceful mind at death influences the rebirth character. Kong, his wife, told Sun to practice meditation and perform *A-ho-si* or forgive himself for harm he might have done to others each night when he went bed, so his *winjan* (soul) would not take all the demerit activities of this life to the next.

Settling Personal and Social Affairs and Resolving Conflicts. When their loved ones were approaching death, families attempted to ensure that the wishes of their loved ones were met and helped them complete unfinished business. Families also asked relatives and friends to visit participants. Doing so provided opportunities for participants and their relatives to resolve feeling of grief, guilt, anger, and conflict, and provided time for forgiveness and saying good-bye. These caring activities also aimed to settle karmic account of the patients. Families believed that doing so would lead the *winjan* (soul) of the dying to better rebirth.

Dressing the Body of the Dead. At the moment of death, karmic activities also prepared the person for the next life. In general the mortuary rite started at the time the person died. Families dressed up the deceased in a beautiful suit. They put money in a pocket, or, in some cases, in the mouth of the deceased, while some personal effects were placed in the coffin. According to informants, the money would be used to buy the way to heaven and the effects provide necessities once there. The dressing of the dead body was commonly performed either by the families or nurses at home or hospital. After being dressed, the corpse was taken to the temple.

Bathing the Body. At the temple the family, relatives and friends bathed the corpse. This ritual was achieved by pouring water on the right hand. During the bathing rite, families said that the living pay respect to and do *A-ho-si* (ask forgiveness of) the dead. As Mai, a wife, said:

Whatever he had done negatively to me, I forgave him. I don't want to blame him. It is like I do *A-ho-si* to him ... because if I blame him, it [the consequence of blaming] will rebound on me. Like other Buddhists, I tried to let it go ... because if we keep thinking about his mistreatment of me it means that he will repay me for this demerit acts in the next life or else. Then his karma will not be finite and his life cycle will not end.

Families believed that the wheel of karma connected two lives. Mai believed that if she blamed her husband for his mistreatment of her in the past the consequences would also affect her own karmic state. In order to conquer and terminate the wheel of bad karma, Mai decided to forgive all mistreatment she had suffered from Pon.

Arranging the Funeral and Cremation. After completing this ritual act, *A-ho-si*, the hands were set in the worshipping position and flowers and a candle were placed in the hands. Families believed that these flowers and candles were used for worshipping Buddha in heaven. One informant said to the deceased that 'You have to hold these flowers along way that you go until you meet the Buddha. Then, you give it to him. If you meet someone while you are walking, do not give or sell these flowers to them.' The deceased was finally put in a coffin, with head pointing west as a guide to the next world. In this study, the corpses of participants were kept for about three to seven days. Monks led the funeral and cremation ceremonies.

All chants in the funeral and cremation served two purposes. Firstly, they created a balance between merit and demerit and drove away the evil effects of the deceased. Secondly, chants served to impress on the living the impermanence of life and enable them to free themselves from clinging to the memories of the deceased. Detachment and the capacity to maintain faith is a central part of the Buddhist philosophy of a harmonious life.

After the cremation, the families collected the ashes and engaged in merit-making activities such as giving alms to the monks. Families believed that they could transfer this merit to the *winjan* (soul) of the deceased, as families believed that they were now alive in other world.

The deceased was finally put in a coffin, with head pointing west as a guide to the next world.

Managing Grief and Bereavement. The death of their loved ones brought about the greatest loss to families. Although families remained connected by their emotional bonds with their loved ones, they attempted to manage and heal their grief and bereavement by their belief in karma. This enabled them to construct a new reality concerning life and death. As Tan elaborated on her acceptance of the death of her daughter:

> She passed away already. She will not reverse to be alive. I still have to live and earn a living. What can I do? She will not return to us. She lives in different world from where I live now. Her life does not relate to us now. We are sad and thinking of her but ... We have to accept. Although we cry, we can cry until it reaches to one level. Whatever we want to do, we cannot do it, except we die with her. This is what I think. It is natural. ... I still think of her. ... But I get used to it. I sometimes cry. ... Because she has passed away already, so I don't know how we could call her back. We cannot help her to be alive again.

These women managed their emotional distress by examining their own experiences through understanding of the law of karma. The death of their loved one meant the end of their suffering and karma in this life ('She passed away already') while the families had to go on living and deal with their own karma in this world ('I still have to live and earn a living'). Families perceived that they had done their best while their loved one was alive. They believed that the meritorious acts they performed would support the person to be reborn in a higher and better status.

After the cremation of San, Tan believed that San was in heaven. This belief was evident by following excerpts such as 'She has never appeared to us since she passed away', and 'San died with merit. You see, her cremation was performed smoothly. We didn't owe money to anyone to manage her cremation. It was all paid with her money. When she died, she didn't owe others. She lives happily now.' The capacity to pay for a well-conducted funeral was seen as a way of ensuring that the deceased went to heaven. These beliefs were important in the management of grief and bereavement.

In addition to managing grief and bereavement, these women believed that feeling sad was due to clinging to their loved one's death and this caused suffering to them. They therefore attempted to detach their feeling from the person as indicated in the quotation 'She lives in different world from where we live now. Her life does not relate to us.' By overcoming attachment through a process of detachment this woman's suffering was relieved.

The death of their loved one meant the end of their suffering and karma in this life ('She passed away already') while the families had to go on living and deal with their own karma in this world.

Discussion

The findings from this study reveal that religious belief played a significant part in the quest for meaning of the families caring for the dying person with AIDS. While a diagnosis of AIDS destroyed their hope for a cure, the belief in karma maintained hope for a spiritual healing. AIDS brought great suffering to these families but medical reality did not help them make sense of the situation. As a consequence, they perceived that the situation was out of their control. Understanding AIDS in Karmic terms enabled the families to give their suffering a name. To call their suffering karma created a new relationship between themselves and their experiences. Families were able to link their past to the present and anticipate the future. They perceived that they had bad karma from their previous life and so it was inevitable that they would receive the fruit of their own karma in this life. Families attempted to redress the suffering of the dying person in the next life and their own in this life. This cause and effect of karmic relationships therefore influenced them to correct their present actions and to perform and cultivate good deeds. Hence it could be said that the religious faith or karma stories worked as 'a moral opportunity to set right what was wrong or incomplete'. . . . The religious faith also helped them to regain control over their lives. Families gradually realised a sense of purpose by integrating the karmic faith with overall healing and focused on perseverance through suffering at the end of life.

The findings support previous research addressing the role of religion and spirituality at the end of life, and the experiences of families facing life-threatening illness. Families accommodated a religious and spiritual faith and practices into their lives to help make sense out of their experiences and move them forward to life and death. . . . They relied on their religious and spiritual beliefs and practices and used them as coping resources to transcend suffering. . . . It could be said that the transformation of illness experiences to the spiritual journey helped families go on following the death of their loved one. They found a new balance in dying experiences and harmonized their plan of care with their belief system.

In addition our findings support other studies that have documented the experiences of families in caring for the dying person with AIDS at the end of life . . . and key attributes of what constitutes a good/peaceful death in both western and eastern countries. . . . Helping the patients search for a spiritual meaning and purpose of life, balancing merit and demerit acts, preparing the state of mind of the dying, settling their own affairs and resolving conflict, dressing and bathing the dead body, making the funeral and cremation, and managing grief and bereavement enabled them to promote a peaceful and calm death and to prepare the passage to the next life.

The results have numerous implications for palliative nursing practice. Firstly they affirm the significant role of families in providing end-of-life care. Nurses should involve the family in such care, particularly spiritual care for the dying persons. Secondly, as palliative care nurses are expected to provide culturally competent and sensitive care for the dying persons and their families, they therefore should be aware of the importance of religion and spirituality in the dying process. Nurses should assess patients' and their families' religious and spiritual belief and practices. This may be achieved by allowing the patients and their families to share their stories about their religious and spiritual faith. A storytelling approach may be useful for helping them find the meaning and purpose of their experiences. . . . In addition, active and attentive listening without judgment and imposing values and ideas, and reflective techniques are required. Doing so will assist nurses to locate the care of the dying and families in relation to their value system, their own personality, and their social world. . . .

In India and Around the World, Hindus Have Rituals for Honoring the Dead

Lavina Melwani

In the following viewpoint, journalist Lavina Melwani inter-
views Dr. Vasudha Narayanan, head of the American Academy
of Religion and a professor of religion at the University of
Florida. Narayanan describes the ways that Hindus prepare bod-
ies for burial and the funeral rituals traditionally performed for
the dead. She notes that Hindu funerals in America have become
Americanized, with the funerals incorporating Judeo-Christian
traditions. She concludes that funeral rituals are a way of help-
ing people cope with grief.

As you read, consider the following questions:

1. What do immediate family members do before the body is cremated, according to the viewpoint?
2. What does Vasudha Narayanan assert is frequently re-cited both in the United States and in India at funerals?
3. Why do some Indian Americans journey all the way back to India, according to the viewpoint?

Hinduism, like other great religions, has specific rituals for honoring the deceased and addressing a family's grief.

Lavina Melwani, "Hindu Rituals for Death and Grief," Beliefnet.com, February 2003. Copyright © 2003 Beliefnet, Inc. and/or its licensors. All rights reserved. Reproduced by permission.

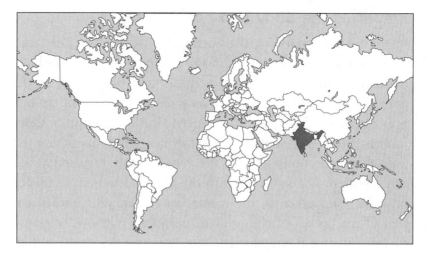

Dr. Vasudha Narayanan, professor of religion at the University of Florida and head of the American Academy of Religion, . . . [describes] Hindu ceremonies. . . .

In most cases, the procedures are conducted almost immediately, within a 24-hour period. When a parent has died and the children live far away, other family members hold the body until the children arrive to do the last rites.

In the place where the [Hindu] person died, a lamp is lit to light the way for the departed soul and water is kept there for its nourishment.

According to Hindu tradition and its sacred texts, only a male family member (such as a husband, father or son) can perform the last rites. However, in some cases women have taken on this role. In Vedic times, there were incidents of the *putrika*—a daughter who could assume the role of a son. In later years, the religious patriarchy interpreted the *putrika* as the grandson, and reserved the conducting of the last rites for males.

Preparing the Body and Family Grief

In most Hindu families, the body is bathed immediately after death, sometimes by women in the family. The ritual marks of the community, along with sacred ash, may be applied on the person's body, under the guidance of the priest who chants holy mantras, which vary in different Hindu communities. Before the body is cremated, the immediate family members put flowers on the body, rice in the mouth (as nourishment for the departed soul), and coins in the hands. The body is placed on a bier and taken to the cremation center. With the exception of the bodies of children and sanyasis [religious beggars], bodies are usually cremated. There are, however, some Hindu communities which practice burial.

When the person dies, the family is in a state of grief. To respect this, no cooking is done in the house until the cremation takes place. "There is a saying that the fire in the house is not lit until the fire in the cremation pyre has gone out," explains Narayanan. "Friends come in with food. There are very specific dietary injunctions also as to what people can and cannot eat, especially the person who has performed the last rites. The food is vegetarian, without onion and garlic. The foods are considered satvic (pure) foods."

In the place where the person died, a lamp is lit to light the way for the departed soul and water is kept there for its nourishment. The next day the ashes are collected and immersed in a river—particularly where two rivers meet; in the ocean; or scattered over the earth in India. "This whole time is one of ritual pollution. There are a certain number of days, depending on the community, after which the family is reintegrated into the society," says Narayanan. "That can happen after 13 days or 40 days—the specific number of days corresponds with caste and community."

While prayers for the dead are common in all faiths, including Hinduism, the introduction of *bhajans* (religious hymns) set to music at a gathering of mourners are a later innovation for Hindus in both India and the diaspora. "Frequently both here and in India you have the recitation of the thousand names of Vishnu [Hindu god]," says Narayanan. "This is particularly common for people from South India. These invocations bring the peace that everyone is searching for in the days after death—peace for the mind and the soul."

The *Shraddha* ritual, in which food and prayers for the departed soul are offered, goes back to Vedic times. These feasts symbolically provide sustenance for the ancestors (rituals with similar philosophies are also found in China and Japan). In Hinduism, they are conducted every month for a year after the death, based on *tithi* (the phase of the moon), and then once annually by the same person who performed the last rites. In recent years, people have substituted other activities in lieu of the Shraddha, such as feeding the poor or giving donations to orphanages. Feeding people in memory of the dead is considered particularly meritorious.

Hindu Funerals in America

"The protocol that surrounds the Hindu funeral in America has changed, the style and texture of the event is far more Americanized than any other rite of passage," observes Narayanan. Indeed, the body is not kept at home as in India but must be taken immediately to a funeral home, and the funeral services reflect Judeo-Christian ones, with mourners watching the rituals take place, while in India these are done in private.

What happens when you don't have a body or just body parts, as in the World Trade Center [September 11, 2001, terrorist attacks] or *Columbia* [2003 space shuttle explosion] tragedies? Says Narayanan, "Whatever part you have you do the cremation with that—it's comparable to when you find a limb during a war or a person is lost in a fire."

Asked if there is anything in the theory of reincarnation or Hindu philosophy that can give solace to the grieving, she says, "What gives solace is the notion of immortality of the

---

A Hindu Funeral Pyre in England Ignites Controversy

A coffin burns on a funeral pyre, as relatives wail their grief. It looks like a scene from the banks of the Ganges [river in India] but this was a field in Northumberland [England] yesterday afternoon [July 2006].

The traditional Hindu ceremony took place after being secretly organized by a race relations group.

Last night police started an investigation into the funeral, which apparently contravened laws restricting the burning of bodies outdoors. . . .

Hindu tradition dictates that bodies must be burnt in the open air.

Andy Dolan,
"In an English Field, a Hindu's Funeral Pyre,"
Daily Mail, *July 13, 2006.*

---

soul. The soul never dies and we have discarded this body because the soul is here and always will be. When you read the verses in the Bhagavad Gita in your time of grief, they speak to you. When you read them in a class or at other times, they are very beautiful. But when you read them in a time of pain, they are almost like a revelation, and it's like a soothing hand on you."

Some Indian Americans journey all the way back to India to immerse the ashes in the Ganges [river] or visit many pilgrimage sites to seek blessings for the departed soul and solace for their own pain. As Narayanan explains, "Rituals give us a way of cathartically dealing with our grief. Every one of the rituals within the Hindu ceremonies is a reality check to help us confront our grief, interact with it, accept it and keep going on—both in life and spiritually."

In Mexico, a Death Cult Thrives

Bess Twiston Davies

In the following viewpoint, Bess Twiston Davies reports on the growth of the Santa Muerte cult. The group worships a saint called "diabolical" by the Roman Catholic Church. Images of the saint show a grinning skeleton cloaked in robes. Her cult is particularly popular with drug addicts and traffickers, and some 40 percent of those in jail are followers, according to the author. Experts believe that the cult and the Mexican fascination with death may be the result of syncretism, the grafting of the Catholicism of the early Spanish invaders onto ancient indigenous religions. Davies is a reporter for the London Times.

As you read, consider the following questions:

1. Which two kinds of Mexicans ask favors from Saint Death, according to writer Homero Aridjis?
2. What event in Nuevo Laredo in March 2009 does Davies cite?
3. What Mexican celebration occurs on November 2?

They seek her dark blessing on the road shrines that line the route to Texas: *la niña blanca* (The white girl), they call her or else, with a touch of grim humour *la flaca* (the skinny one). She's the skeleton, gaunt and grinning, and

Bess Twiston Davies, "Santa Muerte, the Mexican Death Cult," *Times Online*, April 3, 2009. Copyright © 2009 Times Newspapers Ltd. Reproduced by permission.

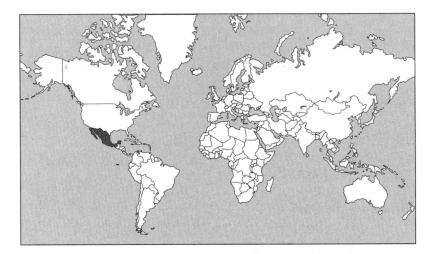

shrouded in veils known as *Santa Muerte,* or Saint Death, who
has become the patron of Mexico's *narcos,* powerful drug
clans engaged in bitter war against the State.

At a time when death by beheading is not uncommon,
narcos turn to *Santa Muerte* to implore protection and "a
good death." Her altars are lined with their offerings: tequila
and rum (she's said to love a stiff drink), tobacco (puffed as
incense over her shrines), and offerings of fruit and flowers:
white roses for healing and red ones for love. Even the candles
are colour coded: green is the colour to ask for justice (or
problems with the law), while gold signifies wealth. Recovering drug addicts favour yellow candles, while black candles
equal requests for total protection, the fulfilment of your
deepest, perhaps darkest desire. Unlike other saints, *Santa
Muerte* is said to make no distinction between good requests
and bad.

Online prayer manuals include petitions for sexual prow-
ess, to stop a wedding from taking place, or getting rid of
troublesome boyfriends as well as help with lesser ills: for
health problems, or to stop children playing truant from
school. In fact, according to Homero Aridjis, a Mexican writer
who has based a short story collection on the theme, two

kinds of Mexican ask favours from Saint Death: "There are those who come to *Santa Muerte* asking for work, health or food, and then there are the wealth, the politicians and the criminals who ask her to grant them revenge or the deaths of other people."

At a time when death by beheading is not uncommon, narcos turn to Santa Muerte *to implore protection and "a good death."*

What is not in doubt is the fervour of her followers. *Santa Muerte* will, assert the commentators on a Mexican blog, "grant whatever you ask, 100 percent and in a short space of time." However, "in the long run, she will make you pay for it, too." Fail to pay tribute, and some say *Santa Muerte* will claim the life of a family member in return. A Chicago-based Mexican warns that his prayers to Saint Death did result in him finding a job—but then his child became seriously ill. There's a price, it seems, for praying to Saint Death.

"It's not that she is bad but sometimes we are," explain the prisoners interviewed on this subtitled trailer for the film *La Santa Muerte*, a documentary narrated by the Mexican film star Gael García Bernal. Up to 40 percent of those in Mexico's jails are, according to this, devotees of *Santa Muerte*, tattooing her emblem onto their flesh. Fifty bodies discovered after a mass shootout in Sinaloa, North Mexico, last year bore tattoos, pendants and rings with the emblem of *Santa Muerte*.

This is a sign, claims the Mexican journalist and regular *New Yorker* contributor Alma Guillermoprieto, of the impact of *narco* culture on modern Mexico. "In the emptiness of meaning that you need to become a mass murderer, you look desperately for redemption and for meaning," she speculates. "You look for them in consumer goods, and you look for redemption in religion," she says.

Saint Death Comes to the United States

Now appearing in New York, Houston and Los Angeles: Santa Muerte. The personage is Mexico's idolatrous form of the Grim Reaper: a skeleton—sometimes male, sometimes female—covered in a white, black or red cape, carrying a scythe. . . . For decades, thousands in some of Mexico's poorest neighborhoods have prayed to Santa Muerte for life-saving miracles. Or death to enemies. Mexican authorities have linked Santa Muerte's devotees to prostitution, drugs, kidnappings and homicides. The country's Catholic Church has deemed Santa Muerte's followers devil-worshipping cultists. Now Santa Muerte has followed the thousands of Mexicans who've come to the United States.

Steven Gray,
"Santa Muerte: The New God in Town,"
Time, October 16, 2007.

Although described as "diabolical" by the Roman Catholic Church, *Santa Muerte* worship is steeped in Catholic custom. Rosaries are recited at her main shrine, set up in 2000 in Tépito, a rough district of Mexico City, and ordinary working class Catholics pray to her, too. The confusion and the crossover is evident. Believers on the trailer pray an Our Father before ominously "summoning" the "presence" of Saint Death.

Death, various Mexican bishops have been at pains to stress, is a passage, a moment between life and death, rather than an entity deserving veneration and prayer. But her popularity is growing, especially in the violent regions at the heart of Mexico's drug wars. Thirty shrines were abruptly demolished last Thursday by the authorities in Nuevo Laredo, a city that borders Texas.

The *Santa Muerte* cult reflects "the tremendous fear of death in contemporary society," says the bishop of Nuevo Laredo, the Right Reverend Humberto Robles Cota. "All of us, absolutely all of us need an interior sense of security, but people who have pushed God out of the picture will cling to anything to feel secure and are clinging to this cult to get that sense of security," he declares. Catholics "ensnared" by *Santa Muerte* worship are confused, adds a spokesman for the archbishop of Mexico, Cardinal Norberto Rivera. They need (and the spokesman blames the bishops) clearer teaching about their own faith.

The Santa Muertistas have their own bishop, too: David Romo Guillén, who has called for a "Holy War" in response to the destruction of the Nuevo Laredo shrines. He wants *Santa Muerte*'s followers to storm the Zócalo, the impressive main square of Mexico City, and the basilica of that great Mexican Catholic icon Our Lady Guadalupe next Sunday in protest.

Santa Muerte *appeals to Mexicans involved in delinquent lifestyles, who have faith but who feel "unworthy" of the "official" God of the Vatican.*

It won't be the first time Santa Muertistas have held mass demos in Mexico City. In 2005, they took to the streets shouting "We are not drug addicts or criminals," and "respect the right to religion" after the government refused Santa Muertistas legal recognition as a church.

To the outsider, the cult of *Santa Muerte* may bewilder, but an intimacy with death abhorred by Anglo-Saxon cultures is ingrained in the Mexican psyche, according to Octavio Paz, the Nobel Prize–winning Mexican writer. "The word death is not pronounced in New York, in Paris, in London, because it burns the lips," declared Paz in his prescient essay on Mexico, *The Labyrinth of Solitude.* He explained: "The Mexican by contrast is familiar with death, jokes about it, caresses it, sleeps with it, celebrates it; it is one of his favourite toys and his most steadfast love."

Each November 2nd, on the Catholic Feast of All Souls, when prayer is offered for the dead believed to be in purgatory, Mexicans celebrate *El Día de los Muertos*, the Day of the Dead. Traditionally, on this date, Mexicans file into the cemeteries setting up impromptu altars at the graves of their loved ones, laden with the favourite food of the deceased. This, it is often said, reflects the uniqueness of Catholicism in Mexico, a faith imported by the Spanish, and grafted on top of existing indigenous beliefs.

The cult of *Santa Muerte* is seen by some as a legacy of this syncretism: The Aztecs held month-long celebrations for death, immortalised in a God and Goddess Mictlantecuhtli and his wife Mictecacíhuatl who reigned over a subterranean kingdom. According to hearsay (facts on Saint Death are few) the cult of *Santa Muerte* was revived in the 1970s after a farm worker in Vera Cruz claimed he had seen a vision of Saint Death in his hut, and the local priest, appalled, refused to bless it.

Gabriela Galindo, a writer with the online Mexican arts journal *Réplica 21* believes *Santa Muerte* appeals to Mexicans involved in delinquent lifestyles, who have faith but who feel "unworthy" of the "official" God of the Vatican and thus create their own altars and saints: "This is how the image of Saint Death has become in recent decades a symbol and icon of those rejected by the power of the Church and of the State," she says

In the Middle East, Suicide Bombings Have a Religious Foundation

David Bukay

In the following viewpoint, David Bukay argues that Muslim suicide bombers are committed to killing because of their understanding of their religion and the concept of jihad, or holy war. He traces the historical development of Islamic jihad before turning to jihad in the contemporary world. He asserts that many jihadists, including Osama bin Laden and Abu Musab al-Zarqawi, cite the Qur'an as justification for their actions. He concludes that while many Muslims and academics try to assign different motivations to the bombers, Bukay argues that jihad is what moves them to action. Bukay is a lecturer in the school of political science at the University of Haifa.

As you read, consider the following questions:

1. What are four ways a believer may fulfill jihad obligations, according to Bukay?
2. What did Osama bin Laden announce on February 23, 1998?
3. What did September 11, 2001, hijacker Mohamed Atta's last will and testament show, according to Bukay?

David Bukay, "The Religious Foundations of Suicide Bombings," *Middle East Quarterly*, Fall 2006, pp. 27–36. Copyright © 2006 The Middle East Forum. Reproduced by permission.

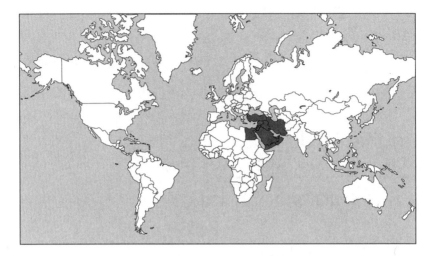

Suicide terrorism has been the scourge of the last quarter century. A suicide bomb attack on the U.S. marine barracks in Beirut compelled Ronald Reagan in 1983 to withdraw peacekeepers from Beirut. Palestinian leaders deploy suicide bombers to force Israeli concessions, and Iraqi insurgents use suicide bombings to derail the new political order. Al Qaeda terrorists attacked the U.S.S. *Cole* in Aden [Yemen] in 2000 and, on September 11, 2001, the World Trade Center and Pentagon. While some scholars argue there is no religious component to suicide bombing—often citing Sri Lanka's Tamil Tigers, who are not Muslims—they are wrong. All Muslim suicide bombers justify their actions with their religion and, more specifically, with the concept of jihad.

A Definition of Jihad

Muslim self-justification of suicide bombing lies in interpretation of jihad. While Western scholars of late argue that jihad refers primarily to internal struggle, Islamic writings feature jihad as physical warfare. Historian Bernard Lewis finds that "the overwhelming majority of classical theologians, jurists and traditionalists . . . understood the obligation of jihad in a military sense."

Islamic jurisprudence has distinguished four different ways in which a believer may fulfill jihad obligations: 1) with faith in his heart; 2) by preaching and proselytizing with his tongue; 3) by good deeds with his hands; and 4) by confronting unbelievers or enemies with the sword. In practice, the first three are part of the *da'wa* (missionary activity), actions that support jihad by the sword.

Martin Lings, a British scholar of Sufism, argues that . . . [the] linkage between martyrdom and paradise was probably the most potent factor that Muhammad brought to the annals of warfare.

Muslim theologians were explicit in the combination of nonviolent and violent jihad to spread Islam. Jihad is central to the Muslim perception of the world, dividing it into *dar al-Islam* (abode of Islam) and *dar al-harb* (abode of war) which is destined to come under Islamic rule. Jihad both purifies the *dar al-Islam* and is the tool to shrink and eradicate the *dar al-harb*. As a doctrine, the aim of jihad is clear: to establish God's rule on earth by compelling non-Muslims to embrace Islam, or to force them to accept second-class status if not eradicate them altogether. Such an understanding constituted one of the main ideological bases of the dynasties that ruled the Islamic world from the late seventh century until Mongol hordes put an effective end to their control in the thirteenth century.

A comparison between the concept of martyrdom in Islam on one hand and in Judaism and Christianity on the other illustrates the emphasis on violent jihad within Islamic jurisprudence. In Islamic practice, the martyr is one killed in jihad. He is entitled to special status in paradise and on Judgment Day. In Judaism and Christianity, a martyr is someone who endures torture and death rather than renounce his or her belief. . . .

Prominent Muslim scholars consider the general jihad declaration against the unbelievers to be crucial to Islamic success. Those who sacrifice their material comfort and bodies for jihad win salvation. By their sacrifice, they obtain all the pleasures of paradise, be they spiritual—the close presence of God—or material. As an additional incentive, Muhammad promised those mujahideen who fight in a jihad war a reward of virgins in paradise. Importantly, those conducting suicide bombings do not consider themselves dead but rather living with God. As sura 2:154 explains, "Do not think that those who are killed in the way of Allah are dead, for indeed they are alive, even though you are not aware." Therefore the prohibition on suicide need not apply to bus bombers or other kamikaze jihadists. Martin Lings, a British scholar of Sufism, argues that this linkage between martyrdom and paradise was probably the most potent factor that Muhammad brought to the annals of warfare, for it transformed the odds of war by offering a promise of immortality. . . .

Jihad in the Modern World

Early interpretations of jihad contributed a theological framework which proponents of suicide bombing adopted. First was the idea that jihad was violent. It was a tool not only to purify the domains of Islam and purge the heterodox but also to defeat non-Muslims. Today, academics and scholars may argue that jihad is peaceful and represents internal struggle, but they either obfuscate or misunderstand that for most Islamic theologians and as described in detail by Islamic historians, the first three nonviolent components of jihad form a larger, more violent aggregate. . . .

Many Islamists are unapologetic about violent jihad. They use Qur'anic interpretation to justify terrorism, suicide bombings, and beheadings. They seek to emulate the aggressive jihad waged by Muhammad and his successors from 626 to 740 in their own struggle. These are the Islamic apocalyptic terror-

A Series of Studies Relates Suicide Bombing to Religious Attendance

In Studies 1 and 2, the frequency with which Palestinian Muslims attended mosque, but not their frequency of prayer, positively predicted support for a specific and extreme example of parochial altruism: suicide attacks. In Study 3, priming synagogue attendance (but not prayer to God) increased the likelihood of Jewish Israeli settlers believing that a specific suicide attack carried out against Palestinians was "extremely heroic." Study 4 demonstrated, in a multinational and multireligious sample, that parochial altruism was positively predicted by frequency of attendance at organized religious services, but not by frequency of prayer. . . .

Taken together, these four studies represent strong support for the coalitional-commitment hypothesis and disconfirmation of the religious-belief hypothesis. Our findings suggest that the relationship between religion and support for suicide attacks is real, but is orthogonal [statistically independent] to devotion to particular religious belief, or indeed religious belief in general. Of course, economic and political conditions may contribute strongly to support for suicide attacks. Our studies concern only the relationship between religion and support for suicide attacks. The proposal that there is some relationship between religious devotion and intergroup violence did not receive empirical support. It appears that the association between religion and suicide attacks is a function of collective religious activities that facilitate popular support for suicide attacks and parochial altruism more generally.

Jeremy Ginges, Ian Hansen, and Ara Norenzayan,
"Religion and Support for Suicide Attacks,"
Psychological Science, *vol. 20, no. 2, February 2009.*

ist groups of today who agree with the idea that jihad is so important that every believer must accept it as a compulsory duty, even when unbelievers have not started it. . . .

Most recent jihadists have relied on Muslim scholar [Sayyid] Qutb [1906–66] to justify their own theories of violent jihad. Abdullah Yusuf Azzam (1941–89), a Palestinian who fled to Jordan after the Six-Day War, adopted many elements of both [Taqi ad-Din Ahmad] Ibn Taymiyya, an early fourteenth-century Islamic scholar who laid the philosophical groundwork for the Islamic fundamentalism adopted by Saudi Arabia centuries later, and Qutb to promote the belief in an inevitable clash of civilizations. He emphasized the necessity of violent revolution through jihad against both secular governments in majority Muslim states and against the West. He is credited with being the first Sunni Islamic figure to instill the Islamic community with a divine myth of invincibility of jihad and terrorism.

Many Islamists are unapologetic about violent jihad. They use Qur'anic interpretation to justify terrorism, suicide bombings, and beheadings.

Islamic Influences on Osama bin Laden

Azzam was a major intellectual influence upon Osama bin Laden and al Qaeda. In his book *Knights Under the Prophet's Banner*, Bin Laden's number two, Ayman al-Zawahiri, identified his organization's goals as *da'wa* and violent jihad against both an "internal enemy," i.e., existing Arab infidel regimes, and an "external enemy" in areas not controlled by Muslims. To Zawahiri, Muslims who accept Western values such as democracy and those who renounce jihad as a means to establish the Islamic state are infidels deserving of death. The Islamic nation, he maintained, would be established only through jihad for the sake of God, compulsory duty vested upon all the Islamic community. He believed that a "Crusader-Jewish" alliance would mobilize all its resources to counter Islamic power.

Bin Laden embraced similar logic. Beginning in August 1996, he used verses from the Qur'an and the Hadith to argue that jihad was compulsory to expel non-Muslims and Westerners from Saudi Arabia. On February 23, 1998, though, he expanded his jihad when, with Zawahiri at his side, he announced the creation of the International Islamic Front for Jihad Against the Jews and Crusaders.

The writings of Qutb also influenced Abu Musab al-Zarqawi, the late leader of al Qaeda in Iraq. Zarqawi peppered his speeches and declarations with verses from the Qur'an and Hadith to demonstrate God's promise of the inevitability of the creation of a pure Sunni Islamic state so long as Muslims fight jihad against the enemies of Islam by jihad. Zarqawi called jihad "the crest of the summit of Islam."

Bin Laden granted Zarqawi permission to kill Iraqi security forces and Shiites in order to achieve a "state of truth" and uproot the "state of the lie." Zarqawi did so with both car bombs and suicide bombers. On May 18, 2005, Zarqawi legitimized the killing of Muslims under the principle of overriding necessity and the victory of jihad. "Islamic law states that the Islamic faith is more important than life, honor, and property," and the Shiites are worse than the Crusaders, he argued. He declared both collateral killing of Muslims and murder of noncombatant non-Muslims legitimate and, on September 14, 2005, declared jihad war on the Shiites. . . .

The violence of contemporary jihad was also apparent in the reaction of Islamists to cartoons published in the Danish newspaper *Jyllands-Posten*. Muslim rioters and Arab and Islamic governments seized upon the contention that it is against Islam to depict the Prophet Muhammad and to argue that the apostates and non-believers should be punished. Violence accompanied demonstrations in Europe and in Muslim countries. By far the greatest number of fatalities was in Nigeria, which is neither European nor Muslim. In London, protestors marched under banners reading, "Slay those who insult Islam," "Butcher those who mock Islam," "Behead those who insult Islam," "Exterminate those who slander Islam," "Massacre those who insult Islam," "Europe is the cancer, Islam is the answer," "Europe take lessons from 9-11 [U.S. terrorist attacks of September 11, 2001]," "Europe you will pay. Your 9-11 is on its way," "Be prepared for the real holocaust," and "Islam will dominate the world." To many jihadists, such threats are literal, not hyperbole. Suicide bombing becomes a legitimate technique to carry them out.

Suicide Bombings and Islam

What is the connection between religious sources of over a millennium ago to the suicide bombings of today? There is a direct link between the jihadists of yesterday and contemporary jihadists. Many jihadists cite the works of Taqi ad-Din Ahmad Ibn Taymiyya (1263–1328), an Islamic scholar born in Harran, in modern-day Turkey, who wrote extensively on the need for jihad and exalted it even above the Islamic obligations of fasting and pilgrimage (*hajj*). He attacked many practices prevalent among Muslims of his time and favored a literal interpretation of the Qur'an. Modern jihadists have used his *fatwas* commanding Muslims to fight the Mongols as precedents legitimizing suicide bombing. [Abu al-A'la al-] Mawdudi, [Hassan al-]Banna, and Qutb have also developed Ibn Taymiyya's philosophy, writing extensively on jihad as the means to fight the reemergence of the age of ignorance, with its tribal savagery and anarchy. They also suggested that the Islamic order can be maintained and protected, if not expanded, through violence.

In recent decades, the Palestinian Islamist group Hamas has embraced suicide bombings to lethal effect. Its 1987 charter shows its intellectual and theological justifications. It cites the Qur'an to promote the idea of Muslim exclusivity and *Hadith* from Bukhari and the *Sahih Muslim* calling for the murder of Jews to hasten the Day of Judgment. More recent exegesis also influenced Hamas. The charter cites Banna's call for Islam to obliterate Israel and is explicit about the violent nature of jihad: Article 13 argues that there is no solution to the Palestinian question but through jihad, and Article 15 declares the necessity to instill jihad in the heart of the Muslim nation.

The 9-11 suicide attacks sparked significant debate in the Islamic world about the merits of suicide attacks. Sheikh Muhammad Sayyid Tantawi, head of Cairo's Al-Azhar, the most prestigious university for Sunni jurisprudence, declared that the Sharia rejects all attempts on taking human life, and Sheikh Muhammad bin 'Abdallah al-Sabil, a member of the Saudi Council of Islamic Clerics and imam at the Grand Mosque in Mecca, decried the suicide attacks on the basis that Islamic law forbids killing civilians, suicide, and protects Jews and Christians. But both Tantawi and Sabil sidestep the question of "martyrdom operations." Because preserving the life of *dhimmis* (Jews and Christians) is conditional to their acceptance of Muslim rule, suicide attacks upon Israelis or Jews and Christians outside majority Muslim countries may be permissible. Indeed, other Al-Azhar scholars, for example, Abd al-'Azim al-Mit'ani, say it is permissible to kill Israeli civilians in the cause of jihad.

Today's al Qaeda splinter and successor groups and their fellow travelers use the writings of Ibn Taymiyya and those influenced by him. The linkage is concrete. They often cite the same Qur'anic passages ... that justified the violent jihad of the seventh century. Religious clerics issue *fatwas* citing them. Perhaps the most prominent of these is Sheikh Yusuf al-Qaradawi who has built upon such interpretations to justify suicide bombing, other acts of terrorism, and the murder of civilians, all in the cause of jihad. He has called suicide bomb-

ing a supreme form of jihad for the sake of God and, therefore, religiously legitimate. Those who object to his ideas he
labels as agents of ignorance. While he argues that the Qur'an
does not allow attacks against the innocent, his definition of
innocence is so narrow as to obviate such assurances.

September 11 hijacker Mohamed Atta's last will and testament shows how deep such interpretations of jihad have pen-
etrated Muslim life as his verbiage and instructions for burial
showed how he believed himself a good Muslim, even as he
participated in an event which murdered almost 3,000 civilians.

Suicide Bombing Cannot Be Separated from Religion

Suicide bombing in the Muslim world cannot be separated
from religion. Its perpetrators believe jihad to be synonymous
with war and mandate Muslims to strike not only at non-
Muslims but also at co-religionists deemed insufficiently loyal
to their radical cause. The ideological basis of such an interpretation has deep roots in Islamic theology, but it came to
prominence with the twentieth-century rise of Muslim Broth-
erhood theorists such as Banna and Qutb and was further developed by their successors. While much of the exegesis developed out of Sunni jurisprudence, the Islamic Republic in Iran
encouraged the phenomenon. Many of Tehran's proxy groups
embraced the tactic.

It is fashionable among Western analysts and academics to
explain away suicide bombing with discussion of "root causes"
that omit religion. Many cite a history of exploitation by
Western powers, Israel's existence, government oppression,
poverty, lack of education, and alienation as reasons why desperate individuals decide to blow themselves up to murder
others. But attention to suicide bombers' own justifications
suggest that, for them, Islam and its call for jihad is the primary motivation.

Periodical Bibliography

The following articles have been selected to supplement the diverse views presented in this chapter.

Andrew Buncombe — "Doomed by Faith," *Independent* (London), June 28, 2008.

Tara Dooley — "End of Life Choices: A Matter of Faith: While Life-and-Death Decisions Are Fodder for Debate, Religious Beliefs Offer Guidance," *Houston Chronicle*, April 2, 2005.

Joe Eaton — "Silent Towers, Empty Skies," *Earth Island Journal*, Winter 2004. www.earthisland.org.

Amitai Etzioni — "Sources of Solace: The Power of Family Ties," *Christian Century*, January 13, 2009.

Globe & Mail (Toronto, Canada) — "Peering down the Tunnel Beyond Death," March 14, 2009.

Doug Hendrie — "The Death of Religion?" *Drum Unleashed*, July 9, 2009. www.abc.net.au/unleashed.

Jane MacDonald — "Let Me Choose the Time and Place of My Death," *Independent* (London), May 11, 2006.

Jenni Russell — "Shorn of the Rituals of Old, Death Maroons Us in Grief," *Guardian*, January 2, 2009.

Susan Schrader, Margot L. Nelson, and LuAnn M. Eidsness — "Reflections on End of Life: Comparison of American Indian and Non-Indian Peoples in South Dakota," *American Indian Culture and Research Journal*, vol. 33, no. 2, 2009.

Kaori Wada and Jeeseon Park — "Integrating Buddhist Psychology into Grief Counseling," *Death Studies*, vol. 33, no. 7, August 2009.

CHAPTER 4

Funeral Practices
Throughout the World

In the United States, Eco-Burials Are Becoming Popular

Valerie Streit

In the following viewpoint, Valerie Streit reports on a new concept in disposing of the dead: eco-friendly reefs under the ocean. A company has devised a way to combine cremated remains with other materials to create the reef. Streit also reports on a second company that manufactures 100 percent biodegradable coffins that can be designed by customers. Eco-friendly burials, using such coffins, in woodland settings are becoming increasingly popular. Streit is a journalist and producer at CNN.

As you read, consider the following questions:

1. In what city is Eternal Reefs located?
2. How will Carole Dunham's daughter find her mother's remains, according to the viewpoint?
3. What state is working with the Green Burial Council (GBC) to expand green burials into a state park, according to Streit?

Carole Dunham, 69, loved the ocean. Last July [2008], she was diagnosed with cancer and had only a few months to

Valerie Streit, "Green Burials: A Dying Wish to Be 'Home for Fish,'" CNN.com, February 17, 2009. Copyright © 2009 CNN. All rights reserved. Reproduced by permission.

live. Dunham knew her last footprint had to be a green one, and she started looking into eco-friendly alternatives to traditional burial.

The concept of "going green" has taken new life in the death care industry as eco-minded companies tap into the needs of those like Dunham.

From biodegradable caskets to natural burial sites, death is becoming less of a dark matter than a green one.

Dunham, an avid scuba diver, chose an eco-friendly company that would combine her cremated remains to form an artificial memorial reef.

Dying is arguably the most natural phenomenon in the world, but modern death rituals . . . are not nature-friendly, according to environmentalists.

"She loved the idea of always being in the water as an alternative to being cremated and scattered," said her daughter Nina Dunham.

Dying is arguably the most natural phenomenon in the world, but modern death rituals—embalming with formaldehyde-based solutions and traditional burial in concrete vaults—are not nature-friendly, according to environmentalists.

Along with its dead, the United States buries 1.6 million tons of reinforced concrete, 827,060 tons of toxic embalming fluid, 90,000 tons of steel (from caskets), and 30 million tons of hardwood board each year, according to the Green Burial Council [GBC], an independent nonprofit organization based in Santa Fe, New Mexico.

"We can rebuild the Golden Gate Bridge with that amount of metal," said Joe Sehee, the council's executive director. "The amount of concrete is enough to build a two-lane highway from New York to Detroit."

Finding an Alternative That Is Friendly to the Environment

Sehee established a burgeoning network of death-care providers that have earned a green thumbs-up in the council's eco-certification program, the first of its kind in the industry.

"We want to reduce carbon emissions, waste and toxins in the death care industry and utilize burial to steward natural areas in the U.S.," said Sehee.

Among the certified eco-providers is Eternal Reefs, based in Decatur, Georgia.

[Eternal Reefs] takes the green movement to sea level by offering a living legacy in the form of underwater reefs used to create new marine habitats for fish and other sea life.

"We're the surf and turf of natural burial," said George Frankel, CEO [chief executive officer] of Eternal Reefs.

The company takes the green movement to sea level by offering a living legacy in the form of underwater reefs used to create new marine habitats for fish and other sea life. The artificial reefs are cast from a mixture of environmentally safe cement and cremated remains.

Eternal Reefs was the logical choice for Dunham, who died on November 3 [2008]. "She liked the idea of being a home for fish," said her daughter.

This month [February 2009], Dunham will travel to Florida to see her mother's reef lowered off the coast of North Miami Beach. Other families will join her, wearing shorts and T-shirts instead of dark suits and dresses. They will have a chance to decorate the reefs with flowers and other sea-friendly mementos.

A brass plaque will help Dunham identify her mother's reef. She intends to visit the underwater memorial by scuba diving there in the future.

"These reefs will be covered up with sea life in a very short period of time, so they make a significant contribution," Frankel said. The reefs last about 500 years, and so far about 300 have been dropped off the coasts of Florida, South Carolina, Maryland, New Jersey, Texas and Virginia.

Biodegradable Coffins

Another eco-provider certified by the Green Burial Council is UK [United Kingdom]-based Eco Coffins Ltd., which allows its customers to design their own 100 percent biodegradable coffins, made from 90 percent recycled grid honeycomb cardboard. The company says the coffins release 72 percent less carbon monoxide in the cremation process compared to a traditional coffin.

"We are appealing to customers to make the responsible choice," said Sophie Dansie, founder and director of Eco Coffins. "The fact that standard chipboard is full of resins and formaldehyde, which is either released into the earth when buried or as emissions when burnt, is really unknown to the general public."

Green Burials Are Good for the Environment

Green burials use environmentally friendly techniques to dispose of bodies and minimize the financial costs associated with funerals. In general, green burials require biodegradable coffins or shrouds if anything is used to cover the body at all. Burial sites are planted with native plants, grasses, and trees. Any practice or substance considered polluting or unnatural is discouraged. Allowing the body to decompose naturally while using as few resources as possible is the goal.

Kelly Joyce, "Green Burials,"
Encyclopedia of Death & the Human Experience.
Eds. Clifton D. Bryant and Dennis L. Peck.
Thousand Oaks, CA: Sage Publications, 2009, pp. 527–29.

The vibrant coffins have even captured some attention in Hollywood. They have a cameo as props in the upcoming [2009] film *Powder Blue*.

An eco-friendly funeral can also help conserve land and protect it from development. The Texas Parks & Wildlife Department is working with the Green Burial Council to become the first state park agency to offer cremation-based green burials. The funds raised from the services will be used to acquire new state park lands.

"We want burials to be more sustainable for the planet, more meaningful for the planet and economically viable for the provider," said Sehee. "We don't want this to be a marketing gimmick that diminishes the social and ecological benefits of this concept," he emphasized.

Couches Made from Coffins

The death care industry, like others, has its share of green hype. While it might be a bit macabre for some, Coffin Couches.com sells eclectic couches made out of used coffins. Founder Vidal Herrera buys unwanted or slightly damaged coffins from funeral homes that would otherwise go to a landfill.

From these discarded materials, Herrera designs artsy Goth couches you might see in a music video or a tattoo parlor. Herrera's clientele includes musicians, actors and others who can afford $3,500 for a couch.

Hype or no hype, the decision is a personal one that ultimately rests with an individual or family. Sehee emphasizes that the Green Burial Council is careful not to diminish anyone's choices or make recommendations about the greenest way to go.

"There are shades of green and people can distinguish one shade from another," he said.

In Uganda, Burial Societies Help Grieving Families

Ben Jones

In the following viewpoint, Ben Jones describes burial societies in Uganda as a social institution. Members pay a fee to the society, and when a loved one dies, the society puts on the funeral. Jones argues that the societies allow people to pay respect to those who have died, and that it is an important part of the fabric of the village. He concludes that while outsiders might not understand the value of burial societies in village life, he believes they are a sign of "meaningful social and political change." Jones is an anthropologist from the London School of Economics and Political Science.

As you read, consider the following questions:

1. What are the societies discussed in this viewpoint called?
2. How long does the typical Ugandan funeral last?
3. What British movement does Jones cite as similar to Ugandan burial societies?

One thing that saddens many of my friends in Uganda is the way we, in the West, bury our dead. The idea that you can go along to the crematorium in town and observe a handful of people saying good-bye to a family member seems

Ben Jones, "The Issue Explained: Death in Katine," Guardian.co.uk, November 25, 2008. Copyright © 2008 Guardian Newspapers Limited. Reproduced by permission of Guardian News Service, LTD.

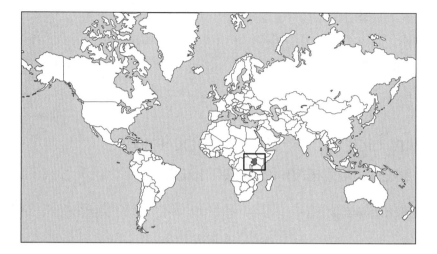

strange to many in Africa. It is taken as a sign that Europeans are increasingly "lost", part of a lonely society that has little respect for the elderly and a less than compelling interest in anything beyond the here and now.

Funerals Are a Community Effort

In Katine, as in the rest of Uganda, funerals are part of a civilised, respectable life. It is important that family members are buried with the participation of the community and with a sense of ceremony. Funerals can be costly affairs and they are organised by institutions known as burial societies. These societies go by the name of akiyo (literally "tears") or amorican ("together in loss"). They are among the most important institutions in the village.

Members pay a joining fee, after which their names are added to the burial book. When a family member dies all the registered members of the akiyo are summoned to a meeting to discuss how the burial is going to be organised. Individuals pay their dues and the money collected is used to pay for the coffin, cloth for wrapping the body and cement for sealing the grave.

The funeral itself typically lasts two to three days. The first day is the burial. Guests gather at the family home, where women busily work in the kitchens, cooking food, preparing beer, or serving and clearing up (women do a lot more work than men). The funeral takes place in the morning or early afternoon. In most cases prayers are said by one of the church leaders in the village. When the burial is over the treasurer reports the income and expenditures of the burial, as well as the remaining balance, which is handed over to the family.

It is important that family members are buried with the participation of the community and with a sense of ceremony.

At this point people are given food, and drink the local beer, ajon. This is the highpoint of the day for many of those who turn up. Burials are part of the social fabric of village life.

What I have described above is an idealised version of what actually takes places. The gender, age, economic condition of the household and reputation of the deceased mean that funerals differ. The burial of Janet Anyango's son would be quite different from that of the village council chairman. And yet there is also a strong belief that all members of the community should be accorded respect when they die. That is why burial societies exist, they offer people that assurance.

Burial Societies Are Established Social Institutions

In the Ugandan village where I carried out research for my book, every household was a member of a burial society. People contribute far more money to burial societies than to the government or the church.

Many in the business of "developing" Africa worry about this, taking a rather negative view of burials and burial societ-

Zimbabwe May Follow West Africa's Example of Coffin Art

In Africa, particularly West Africa, elaborate coffins are built in the shapes of various mundane objects like automobiles or aeroplanes, submarines or even ships.

In West Africa, a coffin or casket is made in honour of the deceased's trade. For an example, if the deceased was a pilot, a coffin or casket resembling an aeroplane would be made. If the deceased was an engine man, a casket resembling a train would be made.

In Zimbabwe the funeral industry has not developed to that stage yet, but developments currently taking place show that we are not far from our West African peers. It is only a question of time.

Philip Mataranyika,
"Zimbabwe: Unbundling 'Myths' Surrounding Coffins,"
Africa News, July 2, 2009.

ies. They think that too much money is spent on funerals. With so many other pressing concerns, why waste money on those already dead? Funerals distract; they take farmers away from the fields, and mean that government offices, hospitals and schools are often understaffed.

And yet, if we look back at our own history we can see that funeral societies are one of the ways in which poorer or working class people in British society have organised their political and economic interests. The Co-operative movement and the friendly societies of 19th-century Britain were formed, in part, around questions of how to pay for a decent burial. The historian F.M.L. Thompson describes a version of Britain that would make sense to many in rural Uganda:

To provide for a decent funeral . . . was the measure of basic respectability; around this minimum core could be built all the other defences against degradation. . . . Getting the means was a matter of resolve, regular habits and social motivation, rather than any particular level of wages. It meant making a regular contribution . . . to an insurance fund that paid out funeral money.

For Thompson, this was the "rise of respectable society"—a sign of meaningful social and political change. And there are obvious parallels between the discipline and organisation of Victorian Britain and the growth of burial societies in rural Teso.

As outsiders looking in on Africa it is important to understand the defining importance of funerals in village life and the level of investment people are prepared to make in burial societies. They have developed without the need for outside assistance or funding, and are more participatory and more democratic than other local level institutions.

Japanese Funerals Are Based on Tradition

Hiroko Nakata

Japan Times writer Hiroko Nakata answers questions about Japanese funerals in the following viewpoint. Nakata describes a typical Buddhist ceremony, including rituals, costs, participant etiquette, and attire. Nakata also reports that several memorial services are held for the deceased at specific times after his or her death. Nakata traces the history of cremation in Japan—the most popular form of disposal of dead bodies in the country. Finally, Nakata notes the ways that funerals and disposal of the dead are changing.

As you read, consider the following questions:

1. According to a Tokyo Metropolitan Government survey, what percentage of respondents said they have participated in Buddhist funerals?
2. What is the proper attire for attending a funeral in Japan, according to Nakata?
3. What does the author say the average funeral costs in Japan?

Funerals in Japan incorporate a unique mixture of religion, tradition, culture, ritual and geography that to the outsider may appear perplexing.

Hiroko Nakata, "Japan's Funerals Deep-Rooted Mix of Ritual, Form," *The Japan Times*, July 28, 2009. Copyright © *The Japan Times*. All rights reserved. Reproduced by permission.

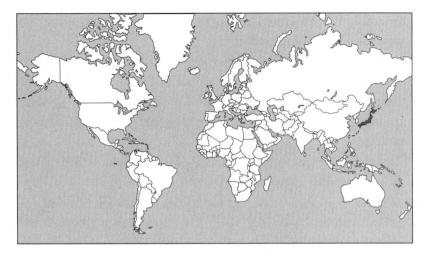

Following are questions and answers about funerals in Japan and related activities:

Do funerals generally have a religious context?

With regard to rituals, most Japanese partake in a mixture of Shinto and Buddhism, with the latter customarily focused on funerals and the departed.

According to a Tokyo Metropolitan Government survey in fiscal 2001, 85 percent of 453 respondents said funerals they have participated in were Buddhist in nature, 4 percent were Shinto and 3 percent Christian. A further 4 percent said they have been involved in nonreligious funeral ceremonies.

With regard to rituals, most Japanese partake in a mixture of Shinto and Buddhism, with the latter customarily focused on funerals and the departed.

Funeral Customs

How does a typical Buddhist funeral ceremony proceed?

The immediate family first keeps a night vigil, or wake, over the deceased on the day of death and generally holds the funeral the following day. Participants can attend either the wake or the funeral, or both.

During the wake and funeral services, participants who are not among the next of kin customarily offer money to the bereaved and burn incense to pray for the soul of the deceased at a temple or other venue where a monk chants sutras before an altar.

After the ceremony, the deceased is often carried in an ornate hearse to a crematorium.

After the cremation, the family and close friends use special chopsticks to collect bone fragments for a cinerary urn, which is traditionally placed in a family grave within 49 days after the funeral.

Rituals can vary, depending on the branch of Buddhism dealing with the deceased.

In recent years, ceremonies have generally tended to become simpler.

Why are rites performed at both the night wake and the funeral the following day?

They are different rituals.

The wake is the last occasion for the next of kin to spend time with the deceased, and the funeral is a ceremony of departure.

Wakes are believed to have originally been gatherings of pupils who talk all night about the lessons from the Buddha when he passed away. These days, relatives and friends stay all night in a lighted room with the deceased, at least as per the practice of the Jodo sect of Buddhism, according to its Web site.

Wakes are also nowadays more convenient for working people to attend than funerals.

Funeral Etiquette

Why do participants offer money to the next of kin, and what is the general amount?

It is customary for people to make a monetary offering to those holding ceremonies, including funerals, to ease the financial burden of such events.

The amount paid often depends on how close the contributor was to the deceased and how old the person is. When a colleague dies, the amount can range from ¥3,000 [yen, the Japanese currency] to ¥20,000 [about U.S. $225]. When parents and siblings die, family members may pay more.

Part of the custom also entails a return thank-you gift for the offering, in many cases a designer towel or dish.

What is the proper attire for attending a funeral and proper way to burn incense?

Basic black suits, dresses, ties and shoes are the norm, and accessories are kept to a minimum. Wearing gray clothing at a wake is acceptable because it is considered a gesture that the attendant felt the death was unexpected.

At many ceremonies, a tray is passed around with incense powder and a flame. The usual practice is for attendants to hold up a small amount of incense and then put it in the flame bowl, repeating the drill one or two more times, depending on the Buddhist sect.

What happens after funerals?

The next of kin and close friends traditionally hold memorial services on each seventh anniversary of the death up until the 49th, although not everyone strictly adheres to this. Similar services are even held one year, two years and six years after a death.

At a gathering at the home of the deceased or a close relative, a monk will chant sutras in front of the family Buddhist altar and then dinner follows.

Cleaning family grave plots on the anniversary of the death or during the weeks of the vernal and autumnal equinoxes are common, as well as during the Bon holiday in August, when people who do not live near their family graves have time off work to make the trip.

Funerals in Japan: Facts and Figures

- About nine hundred thousand deaths occur each year in Japan.

- The average cost of a funeral in Japan is around $23,000—the highest in the world.

- Most funeral services in Japan are Buddhist.

- 99.4 percent of all Japanese dead are cremated.

- The forty-ninth day after death is a traditional memorial day for the deceased in Japan.

- Many companies have a company grave for their former employees in the *Okunoin*, the largest cemetery in Japan.

Compiled by the editor.

The Custom of Cremation

Why is cremation the norm here?

Cremation in Japan springs from Buddhist tradition. The practice is based on the legend that the Buddha's body was burned and his soul transmigrated, unlike the belief of Christians, Jews and Muslims in the Resurrection.

The first recorded cremation in Japan was in 700 and coincided with the arrival of Buddhism in the sixth century. But in the early years, only monks and high-ranking people were cremated because the wood to make the fires was too costly, according to the book *Sekai no Soso* (*World Funerals*), compiled by monk Kodo Matsunami.

The custom spread nationwide only after the war, because of the limited land in urban areas and for sanitary reasons.

Before and during the war, burials were the norm.

By fiscal 2007, cremation accounted for 99.8 percent of all those who died, according to the health ministry.

Big metropolitan areas, particularly Tokyo and Osaka, have local ordinances that require cremation for the sake of public health and because there is not enough land to allow burials.

Rural, remote areas aren't always so restrictive.

Do Japanese Christians seek to bury their dead like many of their Western counterparts, who believe the body is needed for resurrection to occur?

Cremation is the norm for Japanese Christians.

Citing the nation's regulations, the Reverend Tomeyuki Naito, general secretary of the United Church of Christ in Japan, said, "As for us, almost all are cremated."

Although Muslims here are few in number, they have a cemetery that accepts burials in Yamanashi Prefecture run by the Japan Muslim Association.

Big metropolitan areas . . . have local ordinances that require cremation for the sake of public health and because there is not enough land to allow burials.

Funeral Expenses

How much do funerals and related services cost?

The costs average ¥2.31 million, including ¥1.42 million for funeral-related fees and ¥401,000 for catering to attendants and ¥549,000 for monks, according to a survey published by Japan Consumers' Association in 2008.

But the costs depend on the size of the ceremony. Two out of the 314 respondents of the survey said they spent ¥200,000 to ¥300,000, the lowest amount, which another two shelled out more than ¥10 million, the highest.

Are all ceremonies expensive?

No, and the trend is to spend less.

"In recent years, we see the trend because many people become more practical and do not spend wastefully," Kamakura Shinsho, which publishes funeral-related dictionaries, says on its Web site.

An increasing number of funerals are held only by the next of kin. Some go for unconventional funerals and forgo the typical, and pricey, Buddhist trappings.

Some gatherings will play the favorite music of the deceased. Others may show photographs of the dead.

Even the family plot may no longer be the final resting place. Some people want their ashes scattered at sea or from an airplane.

Other Japanese have opted for much pricier excursions, having their remains sent into space, Kamakura Shinsho notes.

The United Kingdom Must Find New Ways to Dispose of the Dead

John Naish

London Times *journalist John Naish addresses the problem of body disposal in the United Kingdom in the following viewpoint. Because burial plots are running out of room for more bodies and cremation is contributing to pollution, city and national governments are seeking new ways to accommodate the dead. Naish summarizes the resomation process that reduces the body to a watery substance, and he describes the process of reusing graves. Finally, he notes a number of novel approaches, including making artwork from loved ones' ashes.*

As you read, consider the following questions:

1. According to Naish, from where does 16 percent of England's mercury emissions come?
2. What is the "lift and deepen" concept being considered for body disposal?
3. How much does it cost to have one's body cryogenically frozen, according to the viewpoint?

They didn't have this kind of problem in Ancient Egypt. As Britain prepares to queue to see the spectacular tomb treasures of the boy king Tutankhamun in London next week,

John Naish, "50 Ways to Leave Your Body," *The Times* (London), November 10, 2007, p. 12, Body & Soul. Copyright © 2007 Times Newspapers Ltd. Reproduced by permission.

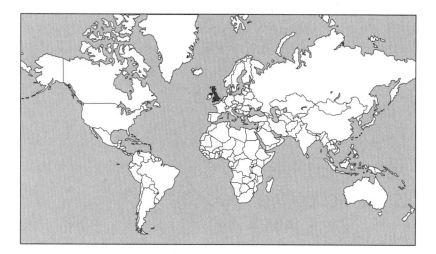

a less heavily publicized funerary gathering will convene in less mysterious and romantic circumstances—in Gateshead.

Our burial and cremation bosses are meeting for their annual conference to discuss a delicate and increasingly urgent question: what to do with all our dead bodies.

Mummification, the arcane craft of preserving defunct pharaohs, won't be on the agenda. But an equally odd-sounding approach will: a way of dissolving humans that was developed for disposing of diseased cattle. Technology may take us from Cairo to cows.

We are in dire need of answers. Traditional burials are in trouble because Britain is rapidly running out of cemetery land. In Greater London, half the graveyards are full and the remaining capacity is disappearing at a rate of 10,000 new interments a year. Crematoriums, meanwhile, face mounting criticism for their high energy consumption and harmful emissions. By law they must halve the amount of mercury they funnel skyward by 2012. At the moment 16 per cent of the country's mercury emissions come from dead people's vaporised dentistry. Expensive "scrubbing" equipment is needed for the chimneys, but not all crematoriums can accommodate it.

The body is dissolved in an alkali solution. New technology may provide radical alternatives. The front-runner under discussion at the Federation of Burial and Cremation Authorities' (FBCA) conference is called "resomation". In layman's terms, it is an accelerated form of natural decomposition. The body is immersed in an alkali solution of potash lye, which is heated to about 160C in a pressurised submarine-shaped steel chamber. Two hours later, you have a watery solution that can be safely poured into the earth and white calcium phosphate, the bone residue, that can be given to mourners like cremation ash. Dental mercury is filtered out. "Scientifically, the process involved is called alkaline hydrolysis," explains Sandy Sullivan, an affable Scot who is pioneering the technique in Britain. "When human tissues are built, elements get bound together by the removal of water molecules. Hydrolysis puts the water back in and unzips the tissue molecules." Sullivan, the managing director of Resomation, the company behind the technique, is presenting his work to the conference jointly with the prestigious US Mayo Clinic, which has been using it for 18 months to deal with the remains of people who donated their bodies to medical research. "For the past decade it has been used in Florida for the batch disposal of the remains of bodies donated for research. Mayo has adopted the same process but in a more mourner-friendly manner—one body at a time, with the body entering the chamber horizontally, just like cremation," says Sullivan.

Traditional burials are in trouble because Britain is rapidly running out of cemetery land.

The basic process has been used with animals since the early 1990s. Sullivan originally worked with a company that developed it for cows that had BSE or had been used for anthrax or smallpox vaccines, as it sterilises as well as decomposes. Now he says his machine is attracting interest and putative orders from America, Canada and "three or four places in Britain".

For the ceremony, the body is placed in a reusable casket that resembles a traditional coffin. This covers an inner coffin made of silk on a metal frame.

This liner is put into the chamber and the silk dissolves. "The majority of the Resomators will be installed alongside cremators as an eco-friendly alternative method," says Sullivan.

The City of London Crematorium is interested in the technology. Dr. Ian Hussein, its director, says: "I'd take one tomorrow. It seems a great invention, but first it must be approved by our board members. One snag is that the funeral directors might be unhappy about not being able to sell mourners coffins." Duncan McCallum, the secretary of the FBCA, agrees that resomation sounds promising. "It isn't releasing emissions into the air and it's not doing the same damage as a burial. It seems to have a lot going for it."

We could go back to re-using graves. Meanwhile, there are important things we could do to address the capacity problems of cemeteries and the ecological impact of crematoria, according to Tony Walter, who runs the MSc in Death & Society at the University of Bath. But they require us to become less squeamishly sentimental and much more pragmatic. First, we could reuse our graves. Until the early 19th century, burial grounds in Europe were reused indefinitely. The wooden grave markers would rot and the plots be excavated: witness the gravedigger in Hamlet, addressing a skull he has dug up.

Bones would be placed in the ossuary and a new body laid in the hole. But the turnover created by Victorian Britain's expanding population meant that diggers began excavating not only bones but flesh as well. Something had to be done. In Britain, the 1850s Burial Acts granted people graves for perpetuity.

Stop cremating people singly. The rest of Europe found a better solution: leasing graves to relatives: the shortest lease is three years in Athens. When the lease expires, relatives renew or the site is reused.

There are important things we could do to address the capacity problems of cemeteries and the ecological impact of crematoria.

Rather than simply empty the holes, a very British compromise has been suggested by the government. It's called "lift and deepen"—the existing grave occupant is dug out, the grave dug down farther, the old occupant replaced and the new occupant placed on top. It's hardly a vote winner but Walter says: "It's been sneaked into the London Local Authorities Act 2007, amid a load of other provisions." Under the new act, councils in London now have the legal right to exhume bodies that have been in the ground for at least 75 years and to practise "lift and deepen". None of the London boroughs has yet tried to exercise these new powers, though.

Walter adds that we could also bury people less deeply. Instead of 6ft, about 3ft under would be much better as that's where there's oxygen and microbes to break down the flesh. "The corpse would be clean after about three years and the plots could be reused. If we used graveyards sustainably, with relatively shallow burial and reuse, the pressure on space could abate."

We could also make crematoria much cleaner, Walter says—if we didn't insist on the deceased being burnt individually, shortly after the curtains close.

"Environmentally we could improve crematoria by putting everyone in the furnace in one batch for, say, 48 hours a week. This would conserve masses of energy because most of the environmental cost is in heating the cremator up. I can under-

---

Scotland Develops Eco-Friendly Graveyards

Everyone in Scotland will have the option of a woodland burial within five years [from 2009], experts predict, as a raft of new sites come under consideration for eco-friendly graveyards.

Scotland currently has seven woodland or natural burial sites, but this is set to rise dramatically in the coming years.

Glasgow City Council confirmed yesterday that it is to turn part of the land at a crematorium in the south side of the city into a natural burial ground as the first of three possible sites.

Jenifer Johnston,
"All Scots to Be Offered 'Green' Woodland Burial,"
Sunday Herald, *August 30, 2009.*

---

stand, though, that people may be unhappy to know that the actual cremation does not happen on the same day as the funeral service."

Going out with a bang

Exploding medical implants are a continual worry for crematoria staff. "Pacemakers have to be removed by a trained expert," says Duncan McCallum, the secretary of the Federation of Burial and Cremation Authorities. "Some implants used to fix broken limbs are very dangerous as they contain pressurised gas. In the cremator they go off with a very loud bang."

Choose your afterlife

Donate yourself

Leaving your body to medical science may not be for the squeamish, but it's like a wholesale form of organ donation.

And it gives medical students and surgeons vital practice. Since 2000, about 629 people have done it every year in England and Wales. The Human Tissue Authority says many donors are former doctors and nurses.

Be a gem

LifeGem of Illinois will extract carbon from your ashes, heat them to create graphite, then press this substance until it yields diamond crystals suitable for pendants or rings.

Freeze!

It costs between £20,000 and £120,000 to have your body cryogenically frozen in the hope that future medics can thaw you out and fix whatever killed you. Two US firms offer the service—the Cryonics Institute and Alcor—and about 161 people are now frozen, with a further 1,000 worldwide signed up, including about 100 in England.

Die for your art

Images for Eternity, another US organisation, creates pieces of art in which a person's ashes are sprinkled on the picture and fixed there with sealant. "It's really beautiful," says the company. "It looks like white sand."

Be plastic fantastic

For thousands of people, donating their bodies to Dr. Gunther von Hagens offers a form of lasting celebrity as part of his Body Worlds show.

Plastination is believed to preserve the body for anything up to 4,000 years.

Form a human pyramid

A German company, Cheops Kolumbarien, claims that the solution to lack of cemetery space is the Egyptian one: pyramids. It has built two in Germany and sold 40 per cent of space inside them. They can contain up to 11 layers and hold the ashes of more than 1,600 cremated bodies. The company says that the pyramids use only about 14 per cent of the space used by current burial methods. A burial spot costs Euro 2,000, (1,390) plus an annual fee of Euro 70.

Periodical Bibliography

The following articles have been selected to supplement the diverse views presented in this chapter.

Max Alexander	"Which Way Out? The Surprising Satisfactions of a Home Funeral," *Smithsonian*, vol. 39, no. 12, March 2009.
Jaye Christensen	"The Eco Way to Go," *Common Ground*, April 2007.
Cheryl Cornacchia	"Ritual Knowledge," *Gazette*, April 19, 2009.
Brenda Power	"TD's Funeral Shamed Him: Tony Gregory's Last Wishes as Carried Out by His Family Showed a Lack of Respect for Mourners and Did Him a Disservice," *Sunday Times* (London), January 18, 2009.
Michael Schwirtz	"In Moscow, No Room for Burials: Lack of Cemetery Space Forces Family Members to Look Outside the City," *International Herald Tribune*, October 7, 2009.
Jerome Taylor	"The Burning Issue of Hindu Funeral Pyres," *Independent* (London), October 14, 2008.
Theresa Vargas	"As Families Opt for Cremation, Industry Expands Services, Choices," *Washington Post*, September 7, 2008.
Arzan Sam Wadia	"Vulture Conservation Project in Surat," *Parsi Khabar*, December 18, 2008. www.parsikhabar.net.
Katie Zezima	"Number of Unclaimed Bodies Increases as Families Can't Afford Burials," *New York Times*, October 11, 2009.

For Further Discussion

Chapter 1

1. According to the viewpoints in this chapter, what are some of the leading causes of death worldwide? What do you think could be done to prevent many of the deaths noted by the authors?

2. The HIV/AIDS epidemic has hit the African continent particularly hard. What are some of the social, political, and medical issues that the world must deal with when confronting the huge number of projected deaths from AIDS facing Africa?

Chapter 2

1. What is the difference between hospice and palliative care? Many of the viewpoints in this chapter argue that such care is a basic human right. What are the main points of these arguments and do you agree or disagree? Be sure to use specific information from the viewpoints to support your answer.

2. A topic of considerable controversy addressed by the authors of these viewpoints is the role of physicians in enabling terminally ill patients to end their lives. What are the major arguments for and against euthanasia, according to the authors of this chapter? Do you think physician-assisted suicide should be legal throughout the world? Why or why not?

Chapter 3

1. Summarize some of the major religious beliefs concerning death covered by the authors of this chapter's viewpoints.

Compare and contrast these beliefs. In what ways do religious beliefs help people cope with death?

2. How do scientific explanations of the death process differ from religious explanations? What role should science play in helping people understand and cope with death?

Chapter 4

1. What are some of the ways that cultures around the world dispose of human remains? Should people consider environmental issues when they plan funerals? What are the environmental impacts of various forms of disposal of the dead, and should people consider these impacts when making end-of-life decisions?

Organizations to Contact

The editors have compiled the following list of organizations concerned with the issues debated in this book. The descriptions are derived from materials provided by the organizations. All have publications or information available for interested readers. The list was compiled on the date of publication of the present volume; the information provided here may change. Be aware that many organizations take several weeks or longer to respond to inquiries, so allow as much time as possible.

African Palliative Care Association (APCA)
PO Box 72518, Kampala
  Uganda
+256 414 266251 • fax: +256 414 266217
e-mail: admin@apca.co.ug
Web site: www.apca.org.ug

The African Palliative Care Association (APCA) is a nonprofit organization dedicated to providing access to and advocating for affordable, culturally appropriate, and high-quality palliative care for those living in Africa. The group publishes articles, reports, and books, all of which are available on its Web site, including "Pain Assessment and Management in Sub-Saharan Africa" and *Pain Relieving Drugs in 12 African PEP-FAR Countries.*

Buddha Dharma Education Association Inc.
78 Bentley Road, Tullera, NSW   2480
  Australia
+612 6628 2426
e-mail: bdea@buddhanet.net
Web site: www.buddhanet.net

The Buddha Dharma Education Association Inc. provides information about the many different schools of Buddhist thought, primarily through its Web site. Information about

Buddhist death rituals and additional resources and links are available on its Web site.

Caring Connections

National Hospice Foundation, Department 6058
Washington, DC   20042-6058
(800) 658-8898
e-mail: caringinfo@nhpco.org
Web site: www.caringinfo.org

Caring Connections is a support and advocacy program of the National Hospice and Palliative Care Organization. It provides free resources and information to people making decisions about end-of-life care and services. Information about end-of-life issues, grief, caring for loved ones, talking to doctors about pain or illnesses, and understanding hospice and palliative care is available on its Web site.

Centre for Death & Society (CDAS)

Department of Social and Policy Sciences
University of Bath, Bath   BA2 7AY
   United Kingdom
01225 386949
e-mail: cdas@bath.ac.uk
Web site: www.bath.ac.uk/cdas

The Centre for Death & Society (CDAS) is the United Kingdom's only organization devoted to the study and research of the social aspects of death, dying, and bereavement. It strives to further social, policy, and health research; provide education; enhance social policy understanding; and encourage community development. CDAS publishes the books *Bereavement Narratives* and *A Social History of Dying* and the journal *Mortality*, which are available on its Web site.

Cremation Association of North America (CANA)

401 North Michigan Avenue, Suite 2200, Chicago, IL   60611
(312) 245-1077 • fax: (312) 321-4098

e-mail: info@cremationassociation.org
Web site: www.cremationassociation.org

The Cremation Association of North America (CANA) is an association of crematories, cemeteries, and funeral homes offering cremation services. It publishes the *Cremationist* magazine. Its Web site contains information, such as links to articles about cremation, surveys of North American attitudes toward cremation, and discussions about the environmental issues of cremation.

Death with Dignity National Center

520 Southwest Sixth Avenue, Suite 1030, Portland, OR 97204
(503) 228-4415 • fax: (503) 228-7454
Web site: www.deathwithdignity.org

The Death with Dignity National Center is a nonprofit advocacy organization that defends Oregon's Death with Dignity Law. Its mission is to provide information, education, research, and support for laws that allow terminally ill patients to end their own lives. The organization's Web site contains articles and links to additional resources.

Green Burial Council (GBC)

550-D St. Michaels Drive, Santa Fe, NM 87505
(888) 966-3330
Web site: www.greenburialcouncil.org

Green Burial Council (GBC) is a nonprofit organization that encourages environmentally sound death care. It encourages the acquisition, restoration, and stewardship of land, and it provides information about finding "green" cemeteries or other funerary services. Its Web site includes links to other sites, articles, and information about the concept of green burial.

International Association for Hospice & Palliative Care (IAHPC)

5535 Memorial Drive, Suite F-PMB 509, Houston, TX 77007
(936) 321-9846 • fax: (713) 880-2948

Web site: www.hospicecare.com

The purpose of the International Association for Hospice & Palliative Care (IAHPC), a nonprofit organization, is to promote hospice and palliative care worldwide. The organization offers training and scholarships for those working in the field. The IAHPC publishes *Getting Started: Guidelines and Suggestions for Those Starting a Hospice/Palliative Care Service*, the journal *Pain and Palliative Care*, and a newsletter on its Web site.

International Observatory on End of Life Care
Lancaster University, Lancaster   LA1 4YW
   United Kingdom
+44 (0) 1524 594976
e-mail: sarah.brearley@lancaster.ac.uk
Web site: www.eolc-observatory.net

The International Observatory on End of Life Care was founded by a sociology professor at the University of Lancaster, England, to undertake research, studies, education, and advocacy for end-of-life care for patients and caregivers. The organization offers publications, books, reports, and journal articles, many of which are available on its Web site.

Bibliography of Books

The following books have been selected to supplement the diverse views presented in this book.

Jane E. Brody   *Jane Brody's Guide to the Great Be-yond: A Practical Primer to Help You and Your Loved Ones Prepare Medi-cally, Legally, and Emotionally for the End of Life.* New York: Random House, 2009.

Eduardo Bruera, Liliana De Lima, Roberto Wenk, and William Farr, eds.   *Palliative Care in the Developing World: Principles and Practice.* Hous-ton, TX: IAHPC Press, 2004.

Pauline W. Chen   *Final Exam: A Surgeon's Reflections on Mortality.* New York: Alfred A. Knopf, 2007.

Peter Fenwick and Elizabeth Fenwick   *The Art of Dying: A Journey to Else-where.* London: Continuum Press, 2008.

Kathleen Garces-Foley, ed.   *Death and Religion in a Changing World.* Armonk, NY: M.E. Sharp, 2006.

Sandra M. Gilbert   *Death's Door: Modern Dying and the Ways We Grieve.* New York: W.W. Norton, 2006.

James W. Green   *Beyond the Good Death: The Anthropology of Modern Dying.* Philadelphia, PA: University of Pennsylvania Press, 2008.

Mark Harris   *Grave Matters: A Journey Through the Modern Funeral Industry to a Natural Way of Burial.* New York: Scribner, 2007.

Glennys Howarth   *Death and Dying: A Sociological Introduction.* Oxford: Polity Press, 2007.

Maureen P. Keeley and Julie Yingling   *Final Conversations: Helping the Living and the Dying Talk to Each Other.* Acton, MA: VanderWyk & Burnham, 2007.

Allan Kellehear   *A Social History of Dying.* Cambridge: Cambridge University Press, 2007.

Rita Langer   *Buddhist Rituals of Death and Rebirth: Contemporary Sri Lankan Practice and Its Origins.* London: Routledge, 2007.

Michael R. Leming and George E. Dickinson   *Understanding Dying, Death and Bereavement.* 6th ed. Belmont, CA: Thomson/Wadsworth, 2007.

Dennis M. McCullough   *My Mother, Your Mother: Embracing "Slow Medicine," the Compassionate Approach to Caring for Your Aging Loved Ones.* New York: HarperCollins, 2008.

| John D. Morgan and Pittu Laungani, eds. | *Death and Bereavement Around the World: Major Religious Traditions.* Amityville, NY: Baywood Publishing, 2003. |

John Powers

A Concise Introduction to Tibetan Buddhism. Ithaca, NY: Snow Lion Publications, 2008.

Steven J. Rosen, ed.

Ultimate Journey: Death and Dying in the World's Major Religions. Westport, CT: Praeger, 2008.

Harold Schechter

The Whole Death Catalog: A Lively Guide to the Bitter End. New York: Ballatine Books, 2009.

Neil Small, Katherine Froggatt, and Murna Downs

Living and Dying with Dementia: Dialogues About Palliative Care. Oxford: Oxford University Press, 2007.

Joy Ufema

Insights on Death & Dying. Philadelphia, PA: Lippincott Williams & Wilkins, 2007.

Christine Valentine

Bereavement Narratives: Continuing Bonds in the Twenty-First Century. London: Routledge, 2008.

Sidney H. Wanzer and Joseph Glenmullen

To Die Well: Your Right to Comfort, Calm, and Choice in the Last Days of Life. Cambridge, MA: Lifelong Books, 2007.

Mary Warnock and Elisabeth Macdonald

Easeful Death: Is There a Case for Assisted Dying? Oxford: Oxford University Press, 2008.

Simon Woods	*Death's Dominion: Ethics at the End of Life*. Maidenhead, Berkshire, England: Open University Press, 2007.
Michael Wright and David Clark	*Hospice and Palliative Care in Africa: A Review of Developments and Challenges*. Oxford: Oxford University Press, 2006.

Index

Geographic headings and page numbers in **boldface** refer to viewpoints about that country or region.